Colophon

©Mathias Jansson (2015)
"Game Art Around the World: From Japan to Cuba"
ISBN: 978-91-86915-19-3
Published by:

"jag behöver inget förlag"
c/o Mathias Jansson
Tvärvägen 23
232 52 Åkarp
SWEDEN
http://mathiasjansson72.blogspot.se/

Print: Lulu.com

All interviews have previously been published at Gamescenes.org 2009-2013.

Foreword

It all started in 2005 when my interest for Game Art awoke. There was not much written about the topic at this time and one question interested me more than others. How did it all start? In the previous volume "The Pioneers of Game Art" I collected my interviews with the pioneers of Game Art. In this sequel I have concentrated on Game Art in different parts of the world and included interviews with a new generation of artists working with video games.

Thanks
First of all I want to thank all the artists, critics and curators etc that have taken time to answer my questions. I know many of you are very busy but still you have taking the time to formulate exciting and detailed answers to the questions.

Special Thanks to Matteo Bittanti editor of Gamescene.org who from the beginning supported the concept with a series of interviews with artists working with Game Art.

Content

Grand Theft Auto and the machinima story (essay) 5

Sean Kerr: Game Art in New Zealand..9

Pippa Tshabalala: Game Art in South Africa 12

Flavio Escribano: Game Art in Spain 15

Laura Baigorri: Game Art in Spain 20

Stephan Schwingeler: Game Art in Germany 24

Isabelle Arvers: Game Art in France 29

Fabio Paris: Game Art in Italy 35

Monica Jacobo: Game Art in Argentina 39

Bart Rutten: Game Art in Netherlands 42

Iris Peters: Game Art in Netherlands..45

Ahmad Zolfagharian: Game Art in Iran...49

"and-or": Game Art in Switzerland 52

Rewell Altunaga: Game Art in Cuba..56

Chris Clarke: Game Art in Irland..61

Johan Löfgren: Game Art in Sweden 64

Olle Essvik: Game Art in Sweden...67

Shinji Murakam: Game Art in Japan 72

Paul Steen: Game Art in Sweden...75

Marque Cornblatt: Game Art in USA...78

Kent Sheely: Game Art in USA 82

Wes W. Wilson: Game Art in USA 85

Benjamin Nuel: Game Art in France 89

Paolo Pedercini: Game Art in Italy *93*

Georgie Roxby Smith: Game Art in Australia *96*

Bruno Martelli and Ruth Gibson: Game Art in England *102*

Grand Theft Auto and the machinima story

The freedom to explore all of a game's territory is one of the keys to the success of the Grand Theft Auto (GTA) series from Rockstar Games. The first game in the series was released 1997. Since then, ten stand-alone games and four expansion packs has been produced for PC consoles and Xbox and PlayStation devices. It's not only the players that love the freedom of the game's storyline—many artists have been attracted to GTA's virtual world and are inspired to explore it further, in their own ways. GTA is a good example how artists today are using different techniques to appropriate commercial videogames for works of art.

But first, I think I need to make a distinction between fan art and game art. As in many popular cultures, there is a lot of fan art connected to videogames that is created by dedicated players. That art can take the form of paintings, stories, videos and so on. But fan art is often only a reproduction of an existing game world. The fan artists are mimicking the aesthetic of the games and are following certain templates created by the fan community. Game art, on the other hand, experiments with and challenges the image and the idea of what a game can be. It can borrow the aesthetic of the game, but it is often critical of that aesthetic. The artists use the game as a platform or interface to explain and explore larger questions of gender, violence, and economic and social realities that are played out in the game world.

One artist that has taken a critical view on the Grand Theft Auto series is the American Joan Pamboukes. In The Enclosed Landscapes series Pamboukes works with C-prints to create impressionist-style landscapes. The pictures are unfocused, with a limited color scale, and in some ways evoke Claude Monet's Rouen Cathedral series, which explored how the light changed on a church façade during the day. In Pamboukes's case, she raises the question of why the landscapes in videogames such as GTA are so beautiful, in contrast to the ugly violence of the story. On her website, the artist states that "I find it ironic that these beautifully serene landscapes were designed to house horrid simulations of unspeakable and appalling violence—a world where thievery, murder, warfare, and prostitution are the order of the day. Mesmerized by these atmospheric digital surroundings, I intended to capture and re-emphasize this intangible, sublime, and fleeting reality,"

The South African artist and researcher Pippa Tshabalala has also worked with photography in her series Telling Death. Here, Tshabalala documented the deaths of different characters in Grand Theft Auto, and asked players to invent stories to explain how they died. Like many other works of game art, Telling Death explores the virtual violence and deaths gamers experience in virtual worlds. The project involves the gaming community, and asks participants to contribute fictional stories about the characters in a way that is also reminiscent of fan art.

It's also becoming common for artists to use videogames as a motif for paintings. Kristoffer Zetterstrand is one example of how artists are transferring the digital image to a canvas). Another example is the Italian artist Stefano Spera. His 2009 oil painting Grand Theft Auto is part of a series of paintings that documents the fictional world of pixels. On the painting's first panel we see a screen with a violent screenshot from GTA, and on the other panel, a child playing the game itself. In this painting Spera is playing with the contrast between the real and the virtual worlds, and the innocent child and the violent society of adults.

Many virtual game worlds let you experience characters, environments, and situations that you would never be able to experience in normal life. For that purpose, the Finnish painter Petri Hytönen spent a year immersed in the virtual world of Grand Theft Auto looking for new inspiration for his art. The results was GTA-SAGA, a series of thirty large-scale watercolors with motifs and situations collected from GTA.

If you think paintings sound a bit anachronistic, I can comfort you that there is also many examples of artists using newer expressions like machinima. In the past few years machinima have become more and more common among artists exploring the world of videogames.

Machinima, a shortened version of the term "machine cinema" are computer animations and movies created inside the games with the help of tools that are often included in the videogames themselves.
Since the early days of Game Art, machinima have been used to create walkthroughs of artistically-modified videogames, which is an important way to preserve and document the work for the future. Machinima has also served as an alternative way for artists to show their works as video installations in art galleries, instead of using a computer with the videogame installed. Today, when many artists are using online worlds and videogames to enact performances, machinima is frequently used to document and preserve these types of temporary works of art. Artists such as Joseph DeLappe and Eva and Franco Mattes, for example, are well-known within the contemporary art scene for their performances in online worlds. DeLappe's Death in Iraq is an ongoing performance piece and anti-war project that takes place within the online videogame America's Army. DeLappe has also been active in Second Life, where he has reenacted Mahatma Gandhi's famous salt march. Eva and Franco Mattes have also created synthetic performances in Second Life, where they have reenacted some of art history's most famous performance works. Machinima have played an essential role in documenting and preserving these performances.

Now, machinima is not only used for the purpose of documentation and preservation, it is also an independent genre of Game Art. Miltos Manetas and Eddo Stern are both considered to be pioneers in this field. As early as 1995 Eddo Stern began to make "machinima" by filming his girlfriend playing Tetris. After that he further developed the art of machinima with epic works like Sheik Attack, 1999, a non-fiction story about the history of Israel, and Vietnam Romance, 2003, about the Vietnam War, both told with the help of scenes taken from different videogames. Miltos Manetas also started around 1995 with a machinima series called Videos After Game. Here you could find such works as Flame, in which Manetas filmed a dying Lara Croft on a Playstation 1, as well as one of the most famous pieces in the series, Super Mario Sleeping from 1997. Today, videogames such as The

Sims, The Movies, Second Life, Half Life, Halo and Grand Theft Auto are often used as sources of artistic machinima.

If we return to the GTA for a short moment, Myfanwy Ashmore, an American artist, has created the video Grand Theft Love Song where the main GTA character Nico Bellic is made to dance in his safehouse. In some ways, the video disarms the violent character by turning him into a puppet forced to dance to the 1927 song Creole Love Call. David Borawski has also created a machinima based on the world of GTA. He describes the 2009 video Burn Out/Erased by the First Rain on the work's Vimeo page thusly: "Burn Out/Erased by the First Rain is comprised of two sequences staged and recorded from within the game GTA – San Andreas. The virtual biker does an extended circular burn out, using the motorcycle's image of freedom and rebellion as a starting point, yet alluding to the repetition and futility of contemporary society."

Today, Game Art has become a broad category that includes Art Games, installations, machinima, paintings and sculpture. If I were to try and define Game Art, I would say that the definition you find in the book GameScenes: Art in the Age of Videogames (Johan & Levi, 2006), edited by Matteo Bittanti and Domenico Quaranta, is still the best: "Game Art is any art in which digital games played a significant role in the creation, production, and/or display of the artwork. The resulting artwork can exist as a game, painting, photography, sound, animation, video, performance or gallery installation."

This essay is a remix of two blogposts previously published on Art21.org.

Sean Kerr: Game Art in New Zealand

Born in Auckland, New Zealand in 1968, Sean Kerr started experiment with video games in the early Nineties. He has worked in various areas of the visual arts, sound/film/video and installation for the past 10 years, and is currently practising as an interdisciplinary visual/conceptual artist and freelance curator.

Your experiments in Game Arts can be traced back to the early '90s. Why video games?
-It is all started when I was at Art School, 1990. To pay my way through Art School I worked in a video arcade parlour. I went to Art School during the day and managed the largest arcade parlour in New Zealand, Yifans, at night. At the parlour I learned about how to fix games and how to play them of course. I started to combined these two interests (art and arcades) together with very simple interventions such as: playing my video art works projected in the foyer of the video arcade. I then started to use some of the arcade interfaces such as: micro switches and coin slots to turn off and on simple sounds and lights circuits. I eventually started to work with computers and incorporated the arcade micro switches and sensor pads by hacking computer keyboards and wiring up the arcade buttons to these keyboards to activate animations, events and sounds.

Was Counterattack, one of your early installations, inspired by Counter-Strike?
-It was just a word play rather that a direct reference, but thinking about it was kind of a first person shooter. It worked by a floor sensor and when the viewer entered the gallery, there was a loud gun shot and a bullet hole would appear on the screen showing a painting of the first four ships, and the counter would go up by 1. The work is really talking about colonization of New Zealand and the site, Christchurch, New Zealand. A larger amount of the 'well off' people of Christchurch came from the first ships and tend to snob people if they are not related to anyone from these ships. The

other thing the title is referring to is the counter on video games, scoring each time you shoot a first four ship.

What was the scene like in New Zealand around 2000, when more and more artists began to incorporate videogames in their works?
-There wasn't much happening then in regards to interactive/ electronic arts. There were only a couple of us that were seriously investigating this area. Terrence Handscomb was the other artist working with game play / narrative and interventions. Towards the end of the 1990s the art scene in New Zealand was still very conservative. The galleries still had problems presenting video art let alone interactive art. Painting and sculpture was seen as a true art practice and the electronic arts were this odd thing on the side. I studied Intermedia at Art school, which had a open approach to art making and this helped me create a practice that is open incorporating sculpture, electronics, moving image, computer, sound, interactives, performance and installation. At that time there was only a few of use in New Zealand pushing an interdisciplinary practice, people like Daniel Malone. This open approach to art practice is now very common.

In the Gameboy exhibition at the Michael Lett Gallery you exhibited retro-game consoles with your own video-games. Can you tell me something about the exhibition?
-Gameboy, references my time at Yifan's video arcade and my childhood experiences at my local video games parlour. The game cabinets are scaled down slightly, so you have to lean over to play them. I always liked the different forms/shapes of the arcade games. The game itself is a simple scrolling game (reference Super Mario a lot), built using tiles and the characters and objects were of past work I have made, such as the The Mountain, Fred (in a box), etc....

You did also participate in the exhibition "Arcadia: Video Games Subvert Art" (2003) at the Govett-Brewster Art Gallery. What was your contribution? How did the public react to your work?

-I presented Bruce, two screens side by side (looked liked square frame glasses) which used video tracking and commented (using the Bruce simpletext voice) on the view watching them referencing using the galleries comment feedback book, where the viewer writes down what they think of the show. Some comments to the viewers were:
- thoroughly enjoyed escaping fantastic.
- you tantilise all my senses.
- being inside you is fully involving different senses and provoking many thoughts.
- you are wonderful, just need a sign with your name on it.
- enjoyed you very much, thank you.
- very groovy.
- you are some what scary.
- you are remarkable.

The interview took place in June 2010.

Pippa Tshabalala: Game Art in South Africa

Pippa Tshabalala lives in Johannesburg, South Africa. Pippa studied Fine Arts and always had an interest in animation and a passion for video games. She completed a Masters degree in Animation and after interning at a game development company she decided to go into teaching 3d animation. In May 2008, she started presenting a TV show called PlayR, on video games, and in December 2008, this expanded to another live show, called The Verge. She also does freelance art and design work, produced and performed live visuals and animation as part of a band called Soft Serve, and currently work as a Creative at Don't Look Down Productions.

Your M.A. thesis was titled "Gaming in Art". What was your research about? What was your main interest at that time?
- I was primarily interested in examining the crossover between video games and traditional fine arts, which was very small at the time I wrote the paper, in 2005. I wanted to examine the different "categories" of game related art that existed, particularly pertaining to experimental and socio-political mods. My case studies were JODI and "Escape From Woomera".

You also produced a series of Game Artworks, such as the fascinating photo series "Telling Death" which features pictures of dead characters from Grand Theft Auto. Can you tell me something about the concept behind this project? Is there any difference between virtual death and physical death, in terms of their aesthetic representation in paintings, photos, and sculptures?
- "Telling Death" branched out from another project called "Simulation". Whilst "Simulation" was a far less interactive work, more of a documentation piece, "Telling Death" attempted to engage with others. I was interested in how others perceived the deaths of these characters, and in the stories they invented for them. Virtual death on the other hand is very interesting for me because I've always compared it in my head to reincarnation - this

concept of saving and respawning. Being able to change our actions in many ways gives us a "clean slate".

Which games, or genres, do you prefer to work with as an artist and why? Where do you find your main inspiration?
- I've tended to prefer the GTA series, but Rockstar in general makes their games very easy to modify and I think that is key. I don't want to have to learn a whole new programming language or circuit-bend anything because that's simply not my area of expertise. I'm often interested primarily in the process of playing, so I like tracking things over time, changing the experience and perceptions people have of something in order to comment on a point and on the viewer's reactions.

Additionally I've always been interested in the transferral of video game media back into "traditional" media, which is why "Simulation" was exhibited as printed photographs as opposed to keeping it purely in the digital realm. I also do a bit of VJing and like to use retro aesthetics and gaming motifs in my that as well. I've played around with OpenEmu in Quartz Composer and really like the idea of using gaming emulators in performance.

What about the Game Art scene in South Africa? How would you describe the climate for videogame based art? Which are the leading artists, and which museum galleries are interested to exhibited this kind of art?
-It isn't very big as far as I'm aware, but as I recently came across a new piece by Nadine Hutton that I think is incredibly interesting. Many of the smaller galleries are open to this kind of art. I've exhibited at David Krut projects in Johannesburg as part of a group exhibition with Eva and Franco Mattes and Bronwyn Millar, as well as blank projects in Cape Town. The smaller galleries tend to attract the right kind of crowd for this work, although with the right proposal I think a group show would do very well.

If you had the possibility to make a wish exhibition with you favourite Game Artists which would you choose, and what make them so important to you?
- I love Brody Condon and Eddo Stern's work so they would definitely have to be a part of it. I'm fascinated by JODI's work and their ability to deconstruct everything (including emails!). I also have an interest in glitches, so their work resonates very strongly with me. I find much of the work emerging from Australian artists of particular interest, especially from artists like Rebecca Cannon and Julian Oliver. All of these artists attempt to push the boundaries of what constitutes art in the context of new media and popular culture, but also don't allow themselves to be stuck in a particular mode of production. That kind of innovation is what is important in our field.

The interview took place in July 2010.

Flavio Escribano: Game Art in Spain

PhD Flavio Escribano is the researcher manager in GeCon. His research interests span videogames, education and training, social inclusion, art and creativity. He founded ARSGAMES (www.arsgames.net) in 2006, a collective research group whose focus is again on Games Studies and Game Art research.

You are the founder and president of Arsgames collective. When did you launch it, and why?
- Yes, indeed, I'm the president and one of the founders of ARSGAMES. In a way it all started by chance. The project started as a conference within the Faculty of Fine Arts of the Universidad Complutense of Madrid. At the time, as part of my PhD programme, I was engaged in situationist interventions in public space, generating artworks against the Intervention of Spain in the Second Gulf War in Irak. They were called SocialCraft and were based on modified levels of the popular videogame Starcraft. My supervisor proposed that we took the idea forward by promoting it through a series of yearly conferences. The first was held in 2006 and during the third one -in 2008- the idea of to found a collective rose supported by the interest of many of the participants. It must be said that in 2006 Spain, the mainstream debate around videogames was pretty much limited to the discussion of the violent connotation of some popular titles. In this context ARSGAMES was born with a broad spectrum of objectives. On the one hand we aimed at promoting innovation in the videogame industry by putting emphasis on experimental essays that blend Science, Art and Technology, which are the object of our own research. On the other hand, by focusing on our past, present and hypothetical future, we wanted to foster the production of videogames that were closer to the Ibero-American culture and further from the Anglo-Saxon and Japanese stereotypes (something similar to Accion Mutante by Alex de la Iglesia or Cronos or Pan's Labyrinth by Guillermo del Toro).

In 2010 you have been involved with PlayLab, a series of workshop about experimental videogames. What kind of artistic videogames can we expect in the future?

-Indeed, after two years of discussion with Medialab-Prado and SONY Playstation we were finally able to align our positions and to launched a call. Although the official announcement was limited to Madrid area we received over 65 proposals from around the world (Austria, France, South America ...), out of which we had to choose eight only. It was amazing to see eight teams and a total of more than 50 people working in coordination with each other and with the tech staff. Luckily the Medialab-Prado's team ensured an excellent best media coverage of the event and supported the documentation of the achieved results through videos and a Wiki. Between November and January another collective called ZEMOS98 and us held a "Game Art" exhibition in Seville called "Over the Game". We tried to be as eclectic as possible. The taxonomy of the Game Art is broad and complex and we wanted to capture at least one representative piece of each of its forms. From Totto Renna to Neil Blomkamp through a variety of local and national artists the public could see how the videogame culture emerges form every artistic disciplines and it is beginning to shape its own language, a language which is rich both in terms of form and content. In my perspective, the future lies in the convergence, that is, in an age where every human experience becomes "playable". To talk about the end of the videogame era would not be appropriate, rather we might say that we are entering into a kind of new post-video game era where borders are being transcended. I think our society will gradually evolve (with crisis or not) towards a leisure society where neo-capitalism will break the difference between play and work (and will force a merger between the first, second and third place as Oldenburg would say). I see two branches in the context of Game Art: The argumentative and critical branch and another branch from the side of the industry to achieve a high level of technical and conceptual innovations. Undoubtedly the game-videogame concept and the historical context will have greatly influence what is to become the Game Art in the future.

What's your assessment of the Spanish Game Art scene? It seems that Spain is the most exciting place to do game-related art. LABoral Art, Gijon, for instance, has dedicated three major exhibitions to Game Art. Are there many artists experimenting with games? What about museums and galleries? Critics and journalists? What's the general level of interest in Spain?

- Honestly, I do not see any interest in Game Art on the main Public Institutions side. Basically, there is ignorance in terms of contemporary cultural movements because our cultural policies are slow and stuck in the past (in Spain would be unthinkable that a fanzine like "Bondage" was ranked as "special edition" obtaining special privileges at the National Art Library as in London). Institutions like the Museum of Contemporary Art of Reina Sofía have never devoted any exhibition or conference to this phenomenon. The effort made in LABoral Art, Gijon to compile artworks, artists, lectures about GameArt and to document the phenomenon has been one of the best initiatives in Europe (if not the best) in support of artists and groups who are working in this area. Such an initiative has been able to stimulate many new artists to start working on this line in Spain. In my case the inspiration came after visiting the Des-GAMES exhibition at MEIAC Museum in 2001, one of the first pioneering exhibitions of GameArt. However there is large interest in the Game Studies concerning games as art and art works in private or semi-public institutions such as the LABoral, the Fundación Caja Madrid and in minority public institutions Medialab-Prado, the vanished art space Iniciarte (Junta de Andalucía) and Intermediae, where they are involved into theoretical discussion or experiment with new forms of exhibition (Estación Futuro in Intermediae). Moreover, in Spain we have what is perhaps the only regular publication (and printed) on Game Studies in Europe: Mondopixel. Still, in Spain we need: more interest from public institutions, more "game-artists" considering themselves as artists and not merely as hackers or engineers as well as critics able to talk about games in a different way than videogame journalistic tradition from the 90s. In any case the situation in Spain is very difficult considering the reductions of between 20% to 50% in budgets of public cultural institutions.

Do you have any favourite artist(s) working with Game Art, and why?
- There are works that I find amazing, projects with a transcendent power within a semantic framework that only one generation of players can feel and grasp with all their poetic and discursive essence. I am especially fond of Joan Leandre's modified games and videos. I think Leandre is an ahead of his time artists - even more so in the Spanish context. He has a very sound theoretical background. At present, and in relation to the paradigm shift Society-Technology-Videogames, I'm closely following Mar Canet's works across the different collectives he takes part to: Derivart (Art, Finance and Technology) and Lummo. Mar is a multifaceted and untiring artist whose roots spread across different disciplines (art, software development, marketing, graphic design, activism...). He's not only capable of mixing his origins to produce interesting and original artworks, he also has great capacity of leveraging the rules of the Market to give great visibility to his work. Both Leandre and Canet were exhibited in "Over The Game".

When did you interest for videogames begin?
- I did not go to videogames, they came to me and I could not do anything about it. My first game was Starglider when I was 8 year. During the 80s I enjoyed the Spanish Golden Age of Software with internationally successful titles as "La Abadía del Crimen", "Navy Moves", "Narco Police", "Mad Mix Games ..." most of them beautifully illustrated by Alfonso Azpiri . Azpiri succeeded in creating an artistic imaginary based on videogames that reminds me what occurs with the main character from "Dream On" TV Serie and films. When I lived in Badajoz I used to visit the MEIAC (contemporary art museum in the city) and found Antonio Cerveira Pinto's exhibition DES-GAMES. He is partly responsible that ARSGAMES is a reality today.

In your thesis, "Videogame like artistic tool", you investigated the relationship between art and digital games. You are also conducting an extensive research about Video Game Platforms as possible artworks. What are you currently working on?
- I'm a currently writing from a modest public Library down-town in Seville, surrounded by books and video games working on the finalisation of my PhD thesis. I have already concluded what you could consider a Master's thesis. My doctoral research is focused on exploring language-specific aspects of videogames in terms of their symbols, their relationship with other artistic disciplines and cultural practices and/or new kind of artistic practices that the game has caused in our society and which did not exist before. I am also very impressed with the work of the philosopher Beatriz Preciado "Testo yonki" and her conception of the human body (especially female) and gender in this era of genetic engineering, chemicals and cybernetics.

The interview took place in August 2010.

Laura Baigorri: Game Art in Spain

Laura Baigorri's main focus is on Art and New Media. Baigorri combines her teaching experience with research, criticism, curatorial work and development of online projects. She has penned articles and essays on art and activism on the Net, video-art and game art, and the books: Net.art. Prácticas estéticas y políticas en la Red (2006), Vídeo. Primera etapa (2004) and Vídeo en Latinoamérica. Una historia crítica (2008).

Your initial interest was on video art and avant-garde movements. Do you consider Game Art an evolution of Video Art and/or a new form of avant-garde?
- I have done a lot of research on the relationship between video art and net.art. I specialized in the history of video art and I was able to witness the emergence of net.art as an art form as it happened, back in the days. In regard to Game Art, I cannot really say if it represents an evolution of video art - especially because it is so recent - but of course there are many similarities between the two. These new forms of art appeared when artists decided to use new media and appropriate forms of popular entertainment to create their work; in a sense, they are both imitating Marcel Duchamp's strategy with the ready-made: they chose something that was already available and transformed it into a work of art. However I don't believe that Game Art's acceptance has been slow because the art scene is now operating differently than in the 1970s. These days, news travel fast whereas before, it took decades for video art to find its niche and to be accepted, both institutional and commercially. Now, for a new "thing" it takes just a few months. Game art and net.art were quickly accepted by art institutions - with some reluctance yes, but mostly were eager to "discover" this new form of media art - because of its character of "novelty" and because of its commercial implications - games are extremely popular with teenagers, who are not usually interested in art.

You were one of the curators of one of the most important Game Art exhibitions ever staged, Homo Ludens Ludens at Laboral, a

follow-up to GameWorld and Playware. Can you discuss your goals for this ambitious trilogy of exhibitions?
- I worked with Daphne Dragona and Erich Berger for Homo Ludens Ludens (2008) at Laboral Centro de Arte and Industrial creation in Gijón. It featured 32 works created by international artists and a big international symposium that required a lot of effort of preparation on our part. Unlike the two previous macro-exhibitions, Gameworld and Playware, we decided to incorporate works that alluded to such notions of game and play, but were not specific examples of game art, because for us it was important to take into account the historical and contemporary frames; references, connections, and consequences of play. Thus, we incorporate works of disparate artists, e.g. Guy Debord -la derive-, Fluxus -interview with Maciunas talking about art and amusement- and a video of William Wegman - Two dogs & ball(1972)- coupled with Tokyo Arcade Warriors (2005) by Axel Stockburger; also, documentaries like Marcin Ramocki and Justin Strawhand's 8-bit (2006) and Ge Jin 's Gold Farmers (2006).

Overall, they were really impressive exhibitions, all well received by the visitors and by the media. One should not forget that these exhibitions were also fun and interactive. But they did not have a long lasting impact, I believe. The did not produce any big shocks in the system, that is, the art world. At the time, most outlets talked a great deal about our exhibitions and Game Art developed in interesting ways, mostly in non-thematic exhibitions. But as a field, Game Art remains niche.

What happened in Spain after Homo Ludens Ludens? What was the impact of that exhibition on the acceptance and development of Game Art in Spain and in Europe?
-After Homo Ludens Ludens Laboral of Gijón hosted two more Game Art exhibitions, Arcadia (2009) curated by José Luis de Vicente and Playlist (2010) curated by Domenico Quaranta, but there have not been others so far. In any case, I think it is more important that the conversation about games and art continues elsewhere, with conferences, seminars, and workshops. I don't want to underestimate the importance of giant exhibitions. But an

art movement cannot survive without a healthy, ongoing dialogue. Exhibitions are useful for archival reasons, mostly.

The current crisis in both education and in the artworld is complicating everything. It has hard to plan new events as funds are thinner than ever. Spain has dramatically cut most investments for cultural and artistic events. Ironically, this had unexpected consequences, such as the massive promotion of young artists, whose pecuniary demands are much lower than those of established, recognized artists. Let's call it a "low-cost" artworld, think Ryanair, but for the art scene. Blessing in disguise?

I am currently preparing a series workshops on video games (October 2011) for the Universidad Pontificia Bolivariana in Medellín (Colombia,) in a clever formula which brings together an academic - an art history teacher - (myself, in this case), a video game designer, and an engineer. This format has been well received in Latin America and sparked considerable interest in Game Art. Today, Argentina, Peru and Colombia are among the most lively country for this young artform.

What is the role and importance of New Media Art, and especially Game Art, at your own institution, the University of Barcelona?

- At the Faculty of Fine Arts of Barcelona, we have been teaching video art for about thirty years. When I joined this institution, in 1993, it became a specific subject. Subsequently, my colleagues expanded the discipline to incorporate more types of new media art. Now, we offer specific courses on video art, interactive art, robotics, theory of digital art, etc.... In my classes of "final projects", I talk about game art in some sessions. My approach is critical. I don't teach design or production.

What videogames have influenced or affected your personal history as a curator, as an academic, and as a gamer?

- Well, I believe I am a completely atypical case. I must be the only researcher in the field of game art who is not - and never been - a gamer. This is because I am 52 years old and, therefore, I belong to a previous generation. When video games were first introduced in Spain, I was more than 20 year old and, around that time, I was interested in different kinds of experiences. So, the question is: Why do I write about them and why am I interested in games as artistic interventions? Before I answer those questions, let me clarify that I do play relatively simple games. For more complex titles, I rely on friends. I watch them playing, I take notes, I drive them crazy with my endless questions...

I was interested in game art of a collateral form. In 2005, some colleagues of the University of the País Vasco asked me that put in context critically a seminar on the subject, but although I was working in 2002 on the monograph Art and Game in Caixaforum Barcelona, I told them that I had no authority to do so. They insisted, and we finally reached a compromise: I would do an approximation to the game from a context that was much closer for me, the critical art (social and political) context. Thus, my examination in January 2006 evolved into a seminar Game as critic as art which I organized at Caixaforum in Barcelona. A fruitful event indeed: creators and experts shared their experiences during two intensive days leading to subsequent collaborations; these specialist were Gonzalo Frasca (Ludology), Anne-Marie Schleiner (Opensorcery), Rafael Fajardo (Crosser y La Migra), Radwan Kasmiya (Afkarmedia), Katharine Wild (Escape from Woomera), and Flavio Escribano (Arsgames).

In 2007, I produced another thematic curatorial work entitled En la brecha. Videojuegos sobrefronteras e inmigración. (In the gap. Video games on borders and immigration) in the Bienal Arte Nuevo Interactiva07 of Mérida (Mexico) and then I already was expanding the field to all kinds of works of game art because I consider it to be one aspect of the New Media art. In any case, my main interest has always been the artworld, not games.

The interview took place in September 2011.

Stephan Schwingeler: Game Art in Germany

Dr. phil. Stephan Schwingeler (*1979) is a curator, researcher and lecturer. His Ph.D. thesis examines the practices and strategies of Game Art and artistic video game modification from the perspective of art history and media theory. He was the scientific consultant of Cologne's Next Level Conference. In the last couple of years he also was responsible for running the GameLab at the Karlsruhe University of Arts and Design.

Your MA thesis focuses on space and perspectives in videogames, framed through the filter of Art History. What did you conclude?
- Speaking with Espen Aarseth every video game is about space. It is the raison d'être of digital games. Every game is about manipulating configurations of space, which the player mainly perceives in the form of images. I wondered if these kinds of images have an art-historical tradition – and of course they do! Foundation for my research was Erwin Panofsky's influential essay "Perspective as symbolic form" from the year 1927. In this essay Panofsky argues that the technique of perspective, which was invented in the 15th century, is a mathematical-geometrical abstraction from human perception and eyesight. With the means of perspective the illusion of three-dimensional space on a two-dimensional surface is created. The new images we see today in video games have a long tradition but new qualities as well. To ask what these new qualities are is a very interesting question. Currently I am working on my PhD which deals with the medium of the video game as artistic material.

Did you trace the evolution of images from the tradition of Renaissance perspective painting and trompe l'oeil to the emergence of 3D videogames?
- The three-dimensional images we see today in video games are constructed in the same way as a renaissance-artist would have constructed his painting in 1460. Modern computer graphics use the same mathematical and geometrical principles. But of course they use these principles automatically in the form of algorithms. One could say these special algorithms behave very much like

renaissance-painters who paint a very well constructed perspectively correct image 60 times a second or even faster. The technique of perspective could be described as a constructional recipe or an algorithm itself. Besides that, images in video games can synthesise every technique of representation ever invented: be it aerial perspective known from painting or in-motion unsharpness known from photography. In the specific aesthetics of video games we can even see that developers include glitches and errors from photography like the lense-flare-effect to be closer to the paradox thing of mediated reality. In my opinion a large amount of video games do not tend to mimic "reality" but to simulate photographic realism.

A new trend in video games is stereoscopy and recently even auto-stereoscopy. Just like the trompe l'oeil these new images tend to reach out of their frame or reach deeply inside of it. This has a tradition in art of its own to be sure.

But images from video games do not only copy known aesthetics and techniques: these images' new qualities are that they give us the illusion of movement and interaction. As a player I think that can literally manipulate the image, which is always connected to my subjective perception via the means of perspective and its vanishing points. The fascinating thing about this illusion is that I as a player think that the image does exactly what I want. I have power over the image. In my opinion the illusion of power over the image is the core of fun in gaming. I can stare at a virtual wall for hours for example or look wherever I want. With Lev Manovich I like to call this phenomenon "arbitrary perspective".

What are the most interesting videogames in relation to Art History? Which games have changed our own understanding of the world?

- Everybody is talking about REZ. It is indeed a huge milestone considering the convergence of art and video games. But it is little known that REZ has an unofficial predecessor, which is at least equally important. The game Otocky from 1987 by Japanese media artist Toshio Iwai is – as far as I know – the first example of an artist using the medium of the video game as his material. The game is a side-scrolling shooter but also some kind of odd musical instrument producing generative music. What makes Otocky so interesting is that it is a commercial video game produced by a renown media artist outside the context of art. (That resembles Bill Viola's rumoured plans to distribute The Night Journey over the PlayStation Network. Iwai was first!)

By the way: there are a lot of games out there that look beautiful and use every technique of artistic expression known to mankind. But frankly I do not think judging the visual surface of video games as artistic is enough. Just because video games are beautiful and designers have to paint and draw a lot does not mean we are dealing with pieces of art. I think the artistic value of video games can lie inside the very structures of the medium: having the ability to create certain aesthetic experiences consisting of audiovisual interactivity. The synaesthesia created by REZ is a good example for that. The metaphor of struggle created by Shadow of the Colossus is another good one. The best pieces of art using video games as their material (e.g. JODI's work) are literally playing with these aesthetic experiences and often lead them to absurdity.

As a player I personally had the best aesthetic experiences with Tetris, the Super Mario and Zelda series and Street Fighter II. Shoryuken! These games changed my way of seeing the world for sure.

This year you have organised the conference "Next Level: Kunst und Kultur der Digitalen Spiele". What was the goal of this event? What were the highlights?

-The conference was organised by the cultural department of the government of North Rhine-Westphalia (a German "Bundesland" or federal state) together with a cultural organisation called NRW KULTURsekretariat. So it was not an underground thing but a highly official event. We tried to transport the idea that playing video games now is a cultural technique of its own: a phenomenon deeply rooted in ludic information society. Gaming has a lot of different, culturally important facets that we tried to show: the whole prosumer-culture consisting of modders and machinima-makers organised in huge communities for example. Another aspect is the demoscene, which is strongly linked to gaming as well. Last but not least we can identify a lot of artists working with video games independently. So considering video games to be industrial products for the purpose of entertainment is not enough. We are dealing with a big cultural phenomenon.

One highlight of Next Level was the keynote by Herbert W. Franke who happens to be the co-founder of Ars Electronica in 1979. Franke is not only a pioneer in the fields of computer graphics and digital art but also a renown science-fiction-author and speleologist! Altogether we managed to gather the German experts in the fields of media art, artists dealing with games and a lot of people who just wanted to play: Next Level was not only a conference but also a festival with workshops held by artists and artworks on display. I hope we can repeat the event in 2011. In the meantime I am still writing a small article at Next Level's blog once a week (only in German, though).

What is that state of the German Game Art scene?
-As you know there have been at least two very important exhibitions in Germany between 2003 and 2005. We had "Games. Computer games by artists" in Dortmund. In 2005 there was the exhibition "Artgames" in Aachen. Back then the curators and critics managed to open new roads theorising art and video games. The curator of "Games" – Tilman Baumgärtel – for example wrote some very important texts about the topic, which still receive attention internationally and get a footnote in almost every text I know about the subject.

Today there are artists working with video games like Aram Bartholl or Olaf Val and even institutions like the Academy of Media Arts Cologne (KHM) or the ZKM in Karlsruhe where games play a significant role on a regular basis. Another important example for a German institution having helped cultivating art and games is the Edith-Ruß-Haus in Oldenburg: They gave a scholarship to Israeli-born artist Eddo Stern in 2007 and he developed DarkGame in succession.

In the last couple of years a group of people in Berlin managed to establish a festival called A MAZE. Which is always a good address for art and games. The events range from parties with renown DJs to symposia with personalities like Julian Oliver and Eric Zimmerman. Even Ralph Baer showed up once! Another important institution would be the Computerspiele Museum Berlin. Director Andreas Lange opened the first permanent exhibition about the culture of digital games in 1997. In the past the museum organised such exhibitions like pong.mythos (2006) and Space Invaders (2008). Later this year the museum will reopen in Berlin situated in a new shiny building! The last exhibition showing Game Art I am aware of was "GaMe!" in the [DAM] Gallery in Berlin. Last but not least there are a couple of journalists who try to establish a kind of cultural game-critique in German mainstream-media like Thomas Lindemann from the newspaper Die Welt. Lindemann laudably deals with digital games the same way as literature, theatre and movies.

You see: there is an active scene, I suppose. The intermixture of art and video games is a topic in Germany but still largely unknown to the average visitor to the museum and the average reader of the feuilleton.

The interview took place in November 2010.

Isabelle Arvers: Game Art in France

Isabelle Arvers is a French new media curator, critic and author, specializing in video and computer games, web animation and digital cinema. She has coordinated ISEA 2000, Paris, and she has curated Video Cuts 2001, Centre Pompidou, Gaming Room Villette Numérique 2002, Paris, Tour of the Web 2003, Centre Pompidou, featuring French and international artists.

You have participated as a co-curator to the Gamerz Festival held each year in Aix en Provence. What was your role and how has the event evolved through the years?
- The festival Gamerz is organised by a collective of game artists: M2F creations.They contacted me when I came back to the south of France and showed me their art related to game culture. We immediately decided to work together because we have the same idea of what game art is and we also have some common roots and interests: parties and graffiti. I think it is important to say that because we are not interested by the idea or the attempt to legitimate the video and computer game matter in front of the contemporary art world. We don't have an elitist conception of what is art and what is not art. What we want to do is the encounter of many different artistic disciplines and practices related to game culture and reverse engineering.

Gamerz is a festival organised as a parcours in the city, based in different art galleries. We show performances of dance or 8-bit music, interactive artworks, photographs, installations, videos, machinimas. We do not want to focus only on interactive artworks but we want to show a large diversity of ludic artworks talking about aesthetics, playability, social or political matters. We are players and we play with art, ideas and concepts. We don't want to have a tight and close idea of what game art is.

We also try to show artworks of young or emerging artists. What is interesting for me as a curator is that M2F Creations has a huge network of artists which are not the traditional "names" of game art. We have a strong collaboration with artschools and artists from the East.

My part in Gamerz is to select international artists. In 2009, I curated the work of Alex Stockburger, a video about goldfarmers and last year I curated two Brazilian artist works: Tania Fraga with an interactive sound game "Danca Maluca" and a very funny and beautiful video of "Rick Castro Super Rick". This year, we want to invite Blast Theory but we are waiting for some institutional funding to be sure to host them under the right conditions... I also curate an annual Machinima program.

What's your take on the French Game Art scene?
- In 2002, I curated an exhibition titled Playtime for a digital art festival at la Villette, between that event and Gamerz, I only had curated game art exhibitions in other countries: Australia, Germany, Italy, Norway... Before Playtime, Laurence Dreyfus Hanout curated a game art exhibition for the contemporary art biennial in Lyon. Then, Margarita Balzerani curated shows about virtual worlds and machinima (The Atopic Festival). Aside from these examples, I could hardly talk about a huge interest for game culture in France in the last decade. On the other hand, our new French cultural Minister decided to raise awareness about video games, so we can hope that the situation will improve. First there is a new interest for a nostalgic part of game culture and some events are organized around the theme of retrogaming in Paris (right now, there is an exhibition titled Musegames at Les Arts et Métiers) I am also preparing a new exhibition tiltled Gameheroes that will be held in Marseille in March 2011. Philippe Dubois who is a collector who I worked with in 2002 for Playtime is also working hard to create a game Museum in France. The artworld is quite sceptical about game art and the artists who were involved with game art some years ago and who are now in the contemporary art scene tend to let the game art for some more "bankable" artworks. I am thinking about the collective Kolkoz who did some very good artworks related to games (Kolkoz.org a game that simulated art collectors flats in which you could destroy everything and especially the art collection) and also to Martin Le Chevallier who did an excellent video about the artificial life in video games Society or a surveillance game: Vigilance 1.0 (2001). Now they are involved in a very

different type of research, unrelated to games. But a new scene is emerging: the more I visit art schools, the more I meet students interested in games. I am really happy about that. Also some game schools like Isarts or Enjmin are producing some artistic games. The frontiers are blurring and we can hope that it will change the perception of immaterial and interactive works in the contemporary art scene. The new names in game art are all artists involved in Eniarof, Gaspard Valerian, M2F Creations, Antonin Fourneau, Benjamin Nuel...

About critics and journalists... Margherita Balzerani wrote an article realted to political games and I am also writing about game art in magazines like Amusement directed by Abdel Bounane. It is a very good and beautiful review about interactivity, digital art and universes, very elegant with texts written by game specialists like all the searchers of OMNSH (Observatory of virtual universes and games) they are anthropologists, sociologists, philosophers, psychoanalysts (Serge Tisseron, Michael Stora). A very interesting group of intellectual writers.

You have also been working as curator for exhibitions with machinima and you have also written a lot about machinima. What kind of machinima are artist doing today and what games are popular to use?

-Right now, I'm working on a new machinima show for the next edition of Gamerz (December 2010). Besides the games and the virtual universes traditionally used to create machinima - The Sims, The Movies, Second Life, Half Life, Halo and GTA, I would add in 2010 the following games : Left 4 Dead, Assasin's Creed and Call of Duty. There is also an important use of dedicated tools like Moviestorm. I really like the work of a Swedish artist William Fink who only produces Machinima with Moviestorm. His movie Phantasmagoria is a very short but intense one. I also enjoy a lot the work of Phil Rice also known as Overman who works a lot with Moviestorm, for exemple his movie "What I like in Xmas..." very good and funny. Lately, the main change in the Machinima world appeared with Second Life which seemed to be the easiest tool for many artists to create Machinima. Last year, I curated a machinima program for the exhibition Gameplay, at Itau Cultural in Sao Paolo in Brazil, where most of the artistic machinima were created in Second Life: "Seeing spot, beeing dots", Evo Szuyuan (Brigit Lichtenegger) NL, Orchestral investigations #9, Gumnosophistai Nurmi (Leif Inge) and Evo Szuyuan (Brigit Lichtenegger) NL Arthole presents : ORIENTATION by Arahan Claveau & Nebulosus Severine, Chantal Harvey, NL, The Body is obsolete, Chantal Harvey, NL, Virtual Gantanamo, Bernhard Drax, US, Maseno Project, Serenity Mercier, CA, Tristeza e Esperança, Carla Broek, BE, My Life as An Avatar", Annie Ok, US.

These works are politically or socially orientated, or they purpose aesthetic and poetic visions. We are far away of the humoristic works of the beginning of machinima. They also offer a critic of these virtual worlds, like in I Mirror of China Tracy, which talks about Second Life as a world where everything is to sold and also questions the virtual identity inside this kind of world and the meaning of encounters in Second Life. But I wouldn't speak about a new trend concerning the use of Second Life but more about some technical necessity and facility. What is interesting is that there is a certain kind of democratization of this movement, not only reserved to hard core gamers and the little community of special effects or game developers, but it is now open to artists, women and youngsters.

You have written an article with the title "Cheats or glitch? Voice as a game modification in Machinima" in VOICE. Vocal Aesthetics in Digital Arts and Media (MIT Press), edited by Norie Neumark, Ross Gibson and Theo Van Leeuwen. What does machinima have to say in the world of 'digital arts and media"?

- I am really happy to be part of this publication directed by Norie Neumark, she was really patient with me and my English! We began this collaboration in 2006 and the book is just out now. It is a book about voice in digital creation. My point is that voice is the only human being part in machinima (besides the fact that characters are moved by humans to create the action). It is voice that gives a certain granularity and "organic" side to digital images. In a movie like "Bill & John" by the French directors KBS Production, the scenes are created with the war simulation game Lock on Modern Combat. There are no characters in this game, you never see any characters moving or expressing themselves, but this movie is super funny and people looking at it lough a lot. It comes only from the voice, which is quite powerful.

The other point in this text is to speak about voice in machinima as a situationist detournement, because voice gives a totally different meaning to images, like situationists were doing, taking kungfu movies to speak about revolution. To give an example, when Alex Chan took the game The Movies to create "The French Democracy" in 2005, he used a game to express his point of view about the French riots and he gave an other voice to all the youngsters which were seen as the devil by the French medias.

What is you personal relationship to videogames? What specific traits of this medium appeal to you?

- I am a player, I play with games as I play with ideas. My background is political sciences and for me games are super powerful. For many generations, it is the first way to learn and to be in the world, it is a way to educate, to have fun and to interact with life and other people. I also see games as a mass consumption object that can manipulate people's mind. For me, games took the place of fairy tales to build young generation's imaginary. So it is for me a very serious question and in all the exhibitions. When I curate I try to promote alternative games or artworks which offer another point of view to this very dominant culture. I always try to promote reverse engineering (Machinima, 8-bit or chip music) all the possibilities offered by a detournement of the initial use of games.

Today, I focus on machinima workshops that I develop towards youngsters,I want to enlarge the capacity of using machinima as a new way of expression, besides hip hop, because it allows you to learn how to write a story but also better understand the power of images and how they are built and how they can manipulate our mind.

Games are for me a way to play with rules and in a way to play with the system, with exhibitions, machinima and 8-bit music it is for me a way to give political messages and to give a critic about consumption and communication society, very powerful because it uses a language that many people can understand...

The interview took place in September 2010.

Fabio Paris: Game Art in Italy

Fabio Paris is a gallery owner - he's the mastermind behind, Fabio Paris Art Gallery (Brescia, Italy), which played (and still plays) a key role in disseminating Game Art in Italy (and beyond). Paris is also a publisher. Publising boos about New Media Art and Game Art under the imprint FPEditions.

In describing the goals of your gallery on the official page, you state that your priority was to showcase art that reveals the "pervasive nature of popular subcultures (from manga to videogames)", which is something that many gallerists/critics - the traditional art establishment/network - tend to dismiss as "non artistic". What is the story behind your gallery?
- I had the privilege of growing up in the 1970s, an extraordinary period of research and experimentation, willing to embrace new artistic languages and challenge to dominant artistic traditions and the social establishment.This particular environment and attitude shaped my own approach to the world of art, moulded my tastes and stimulated a growing interest everything that breaks with conventions and recognized patters. My personal reading of recent art history springs from these influences. I also had the privilege of being a grown man at the dawn of the new millennium, a period in which many of the dreams (and nightmares) of the 1970s appeared to come to fruition

It was then that I decided to do what years of frequenting artists had led up to: opening a gallery. Getting directly into the field, walking alongside the artists, following their paths. It came about on 11 May 2000, in the spring of a new Spring, a new century full of new discoveries: the Digital Era.

For ten years now the Fabio Paris Art Gallery has explored the art that aims to represent the age we live in, where mass information and communications have a powerful influence on our everyday lives. The gallery selects and presents works that talk about the present: a present in which man's relationship with his environment and culture are constantly being redefined by new discoveries, new technologies and new paradigms of thought.

You have exhibited artworks directly inspired by new technologies of communication, e.g. the internet, online worlds and videogames. What was the attitude/reaction of art buyers and collectors to this new kind of art? Has the situation changed in the last decade? If so, how?

- The first real signs of change for my gallery came between 2003 and 2005. At that time this kind of artistic expression was dubbed "experimental art", a label that made it difficult to promote on the market. There were very few galleries in Europe dealing in this kind of art and for years the label kept many collectors away. But in the art world, just like in all other sectors, there are always people with a little bit more foresight than others, and if the gallery survived it is probably thanks to those "pioneering" collectors who were the first to believe in what it was offering.

There is an example I often use in this regard. Think of the new languages in art a century ago, at the beginning of the industrial era, when Dada came into being. At a time when the art market was still bound up with 19th century Impressionism, which and how many collectors were bold enough to buy Dadaist works? Now, a hundred years later, the situation is similar. There is an art form that breaks from the past, an art that reflects the new, digital, hyperconnected world we live in, and there are farsighted collectors who believe in this art, well aware that this is the art of today.

In 2008, I had the opportunity to contribute to Holy Fire, Art of the Digital Age, a show curated by Yves Bernard and Domenico Quaranta for iMAL in Brussels. As a publisher I also published the catalogue. The exhibition, which was part of the collateral programme of ArtBrussels (an important contemporary art fair) set out to debunk the myth that digital art was not collectable, by drawing only from private collections and galleries. It also wanted to raise awareness among collectors and gallery-goers by presenting works that too often circulate only in specialised settings such as electronic art festivals. Many of the works of art on show were already in important collections. It was a kind of consecration to the art market.

How can artists make a profit from works that, in many cases, are ethereal, that is intangible objects? Can net.art and Game Art be collected?
-Growing up in the Seventies taught me not to be afraid of the digital world. At the end of the day, the digital is more "tangible" than conceptual art! The digital can never exist in the form of pure data: software is necessarily channelled by a piece of hardware, whatever that might be. If the work is not in object form (for example an installation or a sculpture like the Self-Disinfecting Machines by Eva and Franco Mattes), it can be sold with its own display, or saved on a magnetic storage medium. Video art has long got us accustomed to dealing with works which are not in object form and tackling archiving issues, and it is no coincidence that many collectors who look to the new technologies have a background in video art and are familiar with the concept of editions.
"Intangible" works can also be translated into objects: digital prints, video, sculptures, 3D prints, etc.. This translation process is often viewed as a compromise, but that is not the case: variability, as Lev Manovich teaches, is one of the key features of the new media. There is no such thing as an original, only versions. Then if we want to get philosophical, everything is sellable, there are no limits. And today there is nothing more intangible than money itself.

Have you experienced episodes where specific artworks violating copyright laws became a problem with corporations /companies that own such content? After all, some artist appropriate commercial videogames in their artworks, images, characters, etc. from videogames or the net and some companies are very protective of their IP. Does that represent a problem?
-Not for me. Appropriation has always been a legitimate artistic strategy. Pop Art showed us how to use media imagery and iconography, taking inspiration from film, television and billboards. I don't see why we can't do the same with the internet and videogames. I can use Coca Cola, why not Super Mario? Obviously the level of appropriation has changed, many works of Game Art use the whole game. What has not changed are the rules of the art

game: the mainstream media churns out characters and settings that strike the collective imagination and become modern-day icons, and artists grant themselves the right to reinterpret these and use them to make something completely different from the original idea that inspired them. In general for me the net and digital languages are a means for freely circulating data and knowledge. Information wants to be free, to quote those who invented the new media, and my anarchic and free-thinking spirit can only go along with them.

You are also a publisher. Your small press, FPeditions, has published a series of monographs on such artists as UBERMORGEN.COM, Todd Deutsch and Gazira Babeli. Why did you start a publishing house? Did you feel that the publishing world has been neglecting Game Art for too long?
-The publishing business is just one of the elements in my artistic and cultural project. It's another way to convey the same contents. It's not for me to say, but the response from readers has shown that the books we have published so far have effectively filled a gap in the market.

The interview took place in August 2010.

Monica Jacobo: Game Art in Argentina

Mónica Jacobo is an Argentinian artist whose practices revolve around the aesthetic and ideological implications of videogames, especially first-person shooters. Visual artist and graphic designer by training, Jacobo has been exploring the porous boundaries between reality and simulation since the mid-Nineties and she was first featured on GameScenes in 2009. Today, Jacobo works as Assistant Professor of Arts at the Cinema and Television department and in the Research Center at the State University of Cordoba, Argentina.

Videogames play a significant role in your artistic practices. What do you find so compelling about this medium? When did you first begin to experiment with digital games?
- I became interested in videogames after seeing a Game Art piece at the 2000 edition of the Transmediale festival. I began working with videogames as media art in 2005. I mostly use FPS titles as they are the most paradigmatic videogame genre in Argentina. FPS are very popular even in low-income urban neighborhoods and in cybercafes. As a woman, I find it interesting to work in that context. Within the FPS genre, I have mostly used the Half-Life engine (based on Quake 2) for artworks like "BSP, Binary Space Partition". I am also keen on appropriating real-time strategy games iconography - a genre that I personally love - and mixing it with the FPS aesthetics. This can be seen, for instance, in photographic works such the "Portals" series and The Sims in the audiovisual work "In search of the perfect bathroom". - Córdoba, Argentina.

In your video piece "00:04:44", you reference a well-known work of art, Joseph Kosuth's "One and Three Chairs" (1965). How did videogame change the relationship between reality and simulation, and the dichotomy between the original referent and its visual replica?
- When it comes to the individual experience of virtual worlds, the boundaries between such categories as "virtual" and "real" have become blurred, if not conceptually problematic. With this work, I wanted to invite the viewer to meditate on the expansion and

dissolution of performed actions between both spaces. What I mean is that for the user moving between those spaces, these actions are perceived as real experiences. Thus, when I insert a real chair in front of the virtual world video, we witness a transformation: a simple, tangible object becomes an evidence of the existence of that world, and simultaneously engage in a conversation with a previous work of art.

"BSP Binary Space Partition" (2007) was specifically created for the Künstlerhaus Büchsenhausen exhibition hall in Austria. Can you tell us more about the genesis of this artwork?
- I made this work for an Artist-in-residence program at Künstlerhaus Büchsenhausen. The space is the room used for exhibitions and lectures in that institution. It was specifically created by an Architectural Studio.
The concept is based on Pierre Bourdieu's notion that the art scene is basically a battle field, a site of friction. BSP is a site-specific video installation. In the video, the room where the exhibition is located is reproduced with the addition of blood marks on an object (e.g: a copier machine). This object was moved into the room just to become part of the video installation, sans the blood marks.
The creation of the video involved several steps. The first was to reproduce the exhibition room with the aid of the Quake (or Half-Life) editor. Then, another (virtual) space made of tunnels was modelled and added. The video begins in this (added) space. Finally, a walk through the created game map was recorded and subsequently edited to produce the final work that was shown at the exhibition.
From the spectator's point of view, BSP triggers questions related to the meaning of space, the creation of memories, and to the consistency of the art spaces. The relationship between the real and virtual spaces and objects, as well as the dissonance between the clean and bloody object, are meant to highlight an object as part of a script different from daily events, like a space that bonds reality and the likelihood of fantasy, or another possible hidden story, sanitizied and cleansed, so to speak, by the actual known history.

In "Portals" (2007-2008) you mix photographs and digital worlds, inducing a sense of cognitive dissonance in the viewer.
- With my "Portals" series, I used public places from Cordoba City, Argentina, that have surreal elements or evoke pre-surrealistic sensibilities. I am equally fascinated by their physical and metaphysical aspects, e.g. the overabunance of concrete in the wrong place with shapes unrelated to any style in the city... Places that can be thought as portals to other places mostly made by the same architect who get the vast majority of the contracts to make buildings and spaces in the city, from public parks to educational environments, like the University of Córdoba. In another, parallel series, "Institutions", I combined photos of museums or local art institutions and FPS iconography (HUD and layouts), to represent the brutal battles fought in the artworld (again, as a reference to Bourdieu). Some of these battles are metaphorical. Other are real.

Is the Argentinian Game Art scene lively?
-The Game Art scene in Argentina is rather small. In the last ten years, there have been a limited number of shows that mixed game and play with Game Art, game art, and game design. I wrote a text about the state of Game Art in Argentina which I plan to translate it into English soon (currently, it is available in Spanish only). There are few artists that sporadically include digital games in their practices. As far as I know, I am the only Argentinian artist who mostly works with videogames.

The interview took place in August 2011.

Bart Rutten: Game Art in Netherlands

On the 6th of October 2011, the Stedelijk Museum in Amsterdam, Holland organized an event called "Do it! Load it!" curated by Bart Rutten. The evening was a result of an ongoing, unique collaboration between the art museum and Submarine Channel, a Dutch multimedia production company. On that date, three new art games were unveiled: Sollmann (Part 1: The Harbour) by Marcel van Eeden and Jorrit de Vries; FLX. by Han Hoogebrugge and Sander van der Vegte; Styleclash – The Painting Machine Construction Kit by Jochem van der Spek. Since 2008, the three artists have been working "undercover" with game designers from Submarine Channel for an ambitious project called "A Split Second":

"A three-year research project initiated by the Stedelijk Museum and Submarine Channel, which explores the concept of artistic authorship within the context of video games by fostering cross-disciplinary collaborations between visual artists and game designers." From the museums homepage.

How did the collaboration between Stedelijk Museum and the production company Submarine Channe begin? Why did the Stedelijk Museum fund a videogame project?

- The Stedelijk has a long, pioneering history in paying attention to new developments in society and media, related to art. The Stedelijk was for example the first museum world wide who introduced the audio tour as an educational tool and one of the first in collecting video art in the 1970s. In 2006 we organized the exhibition Next Level which focused on the influence of games on contemporary art. After this show, curator Marten Jongema, who sadly enough passed away this spring, came in contact with Bruno Felix, one of the directors of Submarine Channel. Together they made this plan to hook up an artist with an interaction or game designer to see how they could influence each other's practice. This was bound to end up in some interesting new, artistic videogames.

Did any of the artists involved have had previous experience with video games?
-Actually, no. None of them had, and that was a very interesting fact. The works of Han Hoogerbrugge and Jochem van der Spek take place in the digital realm but they never worked with a game structure. The artists were specifically selected to give three completely different angles on what a game as a structure or a narrative could be.
"Visual artist Marcel van Eeden and game developer Jorrit de Vries created a short, third-person, 3D mystery game that challenges preconceived notions of the traditional game avatar. In Sollmann (Part 1: The Harbour), the main character is poisoned at the start of the game and gradually loses his ability to see, hear and move." (from Submarine Channel)

"Do it! Load it!" was a very complex event, featuring panel discussions and an exhibition with the new art games. Was it successful?
-We had the three new games in two gallery spaces (Han and Jochem shared a space). The selection of other games, indeed a few a more commercial than the others, where installed in the museum just for just one night, as a kind of intervention. The selection was based on how these games - what we regarded as high quality games - related to the art works on display. We juxtaposed games to paintings and installations withing the museum context, to see what kind of dialogue would ensue. For example: Path was shown next to the exhibition that showed with artists who dealt with the representation of nature. Mirror's Edge was in a room that contained a work by the artist Germaine Kruip, and that work itself is made out of mirrors.

Are we witnessing the beginning of a closer collaboration between artists and game designers in the Netherlands?
-We will see, at the moment we are still enjoying the success of last Thursday – the Load It!-night – and the positive responses to the three new games. Although they still need to be finished in its definitive form, so they can be distributed online, all three are

already acquired for the collection of the Stedelijk Museum. So that is definitely a start. On the special Load It!-night there also was a very interesting panel discussion about your question. It all starts with discussing the subject, because curating video games is not an easy matter. At this moment, with our grand reopening coming up in 2012, it is too soon to commit us to another project like this. But we will keep you posted!

How would you describe the Dutch Game Art scene? What part is the Stedelijk Museum playing in this development?
-Besides Next Level, the Stedelijk show I mentioned earlier, there have been several shows in the Netherlands dealing with games and art. But they mainly took place in a more alternative circuit of artists organizations focusing on new media and digital art like NIMk and Mediamatic in Amsterdam, MU in Eindhoven or Mama in Rotterdam. So in a way I think the Netherlands has already a strong culture on this subject matter. What the Stedelijk Museum will do in the future regarding games and art is not sure yet, but whatever we will do, it will be built on a strong tradition.

The interview took place in October 2011.

Iris Peters: Game Art in Netherlands

Iris Peters is curator and producer at Bosch Art Game. She has a master's degree in art history at the Utrecht University and has curated contemporary art exhibitions across the Netherlands. She have been involved in projects as 'GameQCity, an artistic game experience and 'Playful Arts Event.

You are the Artistic Leader of bART, a mobile platform for contemporary art. You are also the coordinator for the Digitale Werkplaats. Can you tell me more about these platforms and what role they play in the Dutch New Media Art scene, epecially for Game Art?

- bART was the first organization in the Netherlands to develop a major artevent about games & art. In 2011, in collaboration with cultural partners in the city of 's-Hertogenbosch, we set up Game-City, which contained two exhibitions, a conference, music- and film program, festival for youth with a Minecraft LAN-party and more. After that we - that is, my sister and I - were asked to be artistic leaders of the DW, an organization for new media, art and innovation. Now we continue to present artgames by our own initiative or in assignment for both bART and the DW. Also, to engage a wider audience, we set up cross-over projects. This is quite unique in the Netherlands.

In the Netherlands we have an Independent Game scene and a contemporary art or new media art scene, and they are not familiar with each other, they also have different audiences. And within the Independent Game industry there's a division between independent developers and the applied game designers. We are positioned in the middle of this. More and more we see that this platform function and expertise is known and appreciated in both the art and new media scene.

Other artspaces and festivals are picking up artgames as well. For example: we showed Hit me! from New York based designer Kaho Abe, who is now being asked to take part in the large art & technology STRPfestival in the south of the Netherlands and via a gallery we were being asked to show the Playful Arts Festival at an alternative, progressive Artfair in Rotterdam: Art at the Warehouse.

The Digitale Werkplaats is the driver behind the Playful Art Festival in Rotterdam. What is the main concept behind the festival?
- The Playful Arts Festival was launched by bART & zo-ii (Zuraida Buter) with whom we worked on Game-City (2011). The Playful Arts Festival stimulates the cross-over between different fields of play, interaction, art and design. It celebrates playful culture.
The goal of the first edition was to present multiplayer games which bring people together. I think now is the time that people would like to engage more with other people and would like to feel more connected to the place where they are. The selected multiplayer games are a fun experience, so people enjoy art in an active and physical manner. There's lots of talking, exploring, a Dj plays relaxed music... It's all about meeting each other, in an inspiring and open minded setting.

The deadline for the Bosch Art Competition has recently passed. What was the idea behind this competition? What is the connection between Bosch and video games? What criteria did the jurors - Brandon Boyer, Margaret Robertson, Ed Key, Zuraida Buter, and Adriaan's-Gravesande - apply to evaluate the submissions?
- Jheronimus Bosch was a great medieval painter, famous for his paintings dealing with hell and heaven, the seven sins, and full of surreal creatures. "The Garden of Earthly Delights" is one of his most famous paintings. Jheronimus Bosch lived and worked in the city of Hertogenbosch, homebase of bART & DW. In 2016 it's been 500 years since he died and a major cultural manifestation will be organized and as much as possible of his paintings will travel to the city to be exposed.
Jheronimus Bosch lived several centuries before the introduction of electricity or games and it is impossible to say he would have liked games. However, the paintings of JB are so full with imagination and expressiveness that it attracts and inspires game designers. When

asking one of the jurors, Brandon Boyer, to participate in this project he immediately replied that Bosch was one of his first art loves. In my opinion Bosch never lived to see the connection between his art and games/gamers, but there is somehow a natural relation.

What was the response to the competition? Were artists and game designers eager to participate?
- Forty-four game developers and studios subscribed to the international pitch competition for a game inspired by the works of Jheronimus Bosch. Finally sixteen pitched and seven made it to the final, of which six were chosen by the jury and one by the public. I am very pleased with this result. Of course one always dreams for a multiple of subscriptions but given the fact that we are not (yet) well known in the game industry we are very satisfied with the result. The finalists are complementary, with some more experimental and some more classic ideas.

What is your personal relationship to video games and art?
-I have studied art history, and I have been working as a curator since 2003. My relation to video games is rather new. My interest goes out to experimental forms of games, like games as performance, game-installations and physical multiplayer games. I really like the new developments in Independent Games and am really curious to see how this develops, so I continue to bring artgames under the attention of a wide audience.

Holland is investing considerable resources in Game Art - this is kind of amazing considering the recent cutbacks for art and culture funding throughout Europe... How do you explain the peculiarity of the Dutch Game Art scene?
- In recent years there have been many programs to train game developers, in art academies and schools for multimedia and communication. The applied game-industry really flourish, to solve internal complex problems or to learn from, for instance in healthcare and the leisure sector. I think an important factor is also

that games attract lots of younger people and it's important for policymakers to make the connection to younger generations.

The interview took place in February 2013.

Ahmad Zolfagharian: Game Art in Iran

Ahmad Zolfagharian was born in Iran. After Graduating in Print Media at the University of Art in Teheran, he enrolled in an MFA program at Royal Institute of Art (KKH), Stockholm, Sweden. Ahmad is member of /a:t/BrE performance art group. His work has been presented at Mohsen Art Gallery and at Contemporary Istanbul betweeen 2010 and 2011.

When did you interest for video games begin? How are you incorporating game-based technology in your work?
- I grew up with video games. I spent my whole childhood with computers. Developing a video game has always been my dream. When I was studying for my Bachelor Degree in Print Media, I felt that I could not fully express myself with still images as my ideas were dynamic in nature. So I tried to work with animation and films. Eventually, I discovered that the interaction and randomness of computer games have an enormous appeal on me as they are located at the intersection of life and cyberspace. Moreover, due to censorship issues in Iran, cyberspace represents the only opportunity to escape an often oppressive reality. My fascination for interactive games led me to develop my first digital projects, "Under Destruction" and Life".

"A regeneration of Gorillas, a game made in 1988 which could be played on DOS 5 operating system. During Israel's invasion to Gazza, BBC showed images of Israelis rejoicing in their successful bombardment of Gazza and crying in joy each time a rocket hit the target. At the same time, Iranian National Television broadcast scenes in which Palestinians were throwing rockets at Israelis and crying out in rejoice. It was the moment when I truly believed war and struggle has become meaningless for both sides and they are aiming at pure destruction and annihilation and nothing more." (Ahmad Zolfagharian)

What can you tell us about the Iranian Game Art scene?
- There are several artists working with video games as a medium of expression. However, in the Iranian art scene, video games are still

relatively new and the critics don't take them seriously, they tend to dismiss them as "trivial". Moreover, because copyright laws are somehow vague, there is no market for this medium. In short, for many artists, games represent a mere exercise, a form of exploration. They would not be able to make a living, so to speak, thus few game-based artworks are actually shown in galleries.

What was your original intent behind "Under deconstruction"?
- "Under Deconstruction" is a remake of Gorillas, a game made in 1988 which could be played on DOS 5 operating system. It is one of the first game that I played and grown up with it, I began playing this game when I was just seven years old. I can remember reading about the struggle between Israel and Palestine around that time. During Israel's invasion to Gaza, BBC Persia showed images of Israelis rejoicing in their successful bombardments of Gaza and crying in joy each time a rocket hit the target. At the same time, Iranian National Television broadcast scenes in which Palestinians were throwing rockets at Israelis and crying out in rejoice. So, I just find a DOS version of the game, and then I tried to remake it by using Actionscript. I changed some specifications of the game, for instance I added Israel and Palestine flags and animated them. In the original game, when one of the opponent kill the other, he does a little dance. In this game when one of the player destroys a city skyline, both players will dance, and if one of them kills the other, he will dance. I used the idea of wind directional arrow to show the mass media inclination about this issue.

"At the beginning of the game, the player is informed that his task is to find an object which is located somewhere in a labyrinth. However, this information is incorrect and the game actually ends (i.e. reaches 'death point') when the duration of the game equals an accidental amount that the programme each time defines At that point, the labyrinth fades and the path the player has moved along becomes visible." (Ahmad Zolfagharian)

What about the game "Life"?
- At the beginning of this game, the player is informed that his task is to find an object located somewhere in a huge and complicated labyrinth. If he can find that object he wins the game of "Life'. Depending on the time of your life, the objects in the labyrinth will change. There are six levels: infancy, childhood, adolescence, young adulthood, middle adulthood and maturity. However, this information is incorrect and the game actually ends (i.e. reaches 'death point') when the duration of the game equals an accidental amount that the program randomly defines. Then labyrinth fades and the path taken by the player becomes visible. This is inspired by an orientalist idea that the meaning of life is about the path not the so-called "goal".

Art and videogames are closely interwined in your work. Will you continue to explore this connection?
- Game Art's relationship with moving images and video could not be stronger. By adding interaction to my artworks, I'm looking for the audience to spend more time than they would generally spend in a gallery. As an artist, I want to make an audience to have a deeper engagement with my artworks. I can say that interaction between game art and its audience is like a performance art as the audience is part of the artworks. I am still looking for a way to develop a stronger connection with the audience... To me, interactive art and Game Art are the best solution, at least for now. I will definitely continue to explore this area more. As a matter of fact, I am working on a new interactive video game which will soon see the light of the day.

The interview took place in December 2010.

"and-or": Game Art in Switzerland

and-or is an artgroup specializing in media art and gameArt. The group consists of René Bauer, Beat Suter and Mirjam Weder. The group operates since 2001 from Zurich, Switzerland.

What is "and-or", exactly? Who are the members of this collective?
- "and-or "is a Swiss artgroup specializing in media art and Game Art. The group consists of René Bauer, Beat Suter and Mirjam Weder. The group operates since 2001 from Zurich, Switzerland. and-or explores new modes of interactivity and concreativity (*) between machines and their human users. Simple but distinct concepts become game prototypes or playful media art. Digital data is everywhere these days but its impact often is not considered. We make this data and its impact visible to everyone, we question it and open up a discourse on digital boundaries.

For this purpose we often use feeds of constant ideas and thoughts (digital ready-mades) as found in search engines, feeds of publicly available pictures and sounds and various behaviour-patterns of gameplay. Put in a playful perspective, these can easily show you what lies beneath the digital surface and beyond the common limits of communication.

And-or's origin is the media art scene. Some of our projects like Wardive, Sniff_jazzbox and AndOrDada are media art projects created for mobile devices. They capture and transpose communication waves between humans and machines into adaptive and locative games, music or poetry. AndOrDada creates a poem that adapts itself to the area of town you walk through and weaves your friend's names into the poem. Sniff_jazzbox transposes areas of town via names of hotspots in music and generally creates an audible city. Wardive finally is the game version. While walking or driving through town hotspots become enemies and need to be fended off quickly before they destroy your crystal.

(*) Concreativity is a concept of cooperating on a work of art or literature or music etc. whereby each cooperator or partner has a creatve input. The word is not used very much. It was an academic term used by sociologists. We started using it a few years ago to make a distinction to the simpler concepts of collaboration and ccoperation (Beat Suter, and-or)

Gamescape is one of your most discussed works. How did you develop this artwork?
- Gamescape is based on the 80s game Qix, respectively its successor Volfied. The player has to conquest the opponent's dominion. Piece by piece he cuts off territory and diminishes the opponent's freedom of movement. With each cut he adds another floor to a building that may develop into a skyscraper. The basic idea of Gamescape is to make a game's processes visible. Usually a player is not able to backtrack his or her activities in a game. He just gets a result, respectively sees his score. In Gamescape all games of all players grow into cities. Over the last few years more than 25'000 cities with more than 20 skyscrapers each developed - all of them individually played game levels as 3D-cut-outs or 3D-sculptures. This 3D-sculptures by the way can be further used in 3D-software for modelling or cresting new urban scapes in Google Earth. The game shows what hides in games: One day we will play games and while doing this, we will work for others. This is only a matter of time.

And Laichenberg? What is the idea behind this project and how was it made?
- Laichenberg was developed as an answer to the eternal and pubertal question: "What game is the most realistic of all?" We made a game that is more realistic in only one but very important point: The corpses of the killed enemies (frags) do not disappear. It means that this game has a "realistic" defect. This of course leads to problems: After 10 minutes you can hardly move anymore among all the corpses. In the game you slip into the role of a soldier after a nuclear war that can't help but continue his fight as a mercenary in a Tibetan bunker. The game follows a literary text by the famous Swiss writer Friedrich Dürrenmatt (Winter war in Tibet). Deep down in the bunker system soldier 23 discovers his sense of life: Killing! In this respect this soldier is a classic First Person Shooter.

Laichenberg's graphic design adapts Swiss military uniforms from mid 20th century, a time when the Swiss army prepared to retreat to its alpine bunker system. Interestingly enough the elaborate bunker system in Switzerland that even included some production facilities was not prepared to deal with lots of dead soldiers and civilians. There would have been lots of problems, once the killing started

First we wanted to develop a multiplayer level for Laichenberg, but after some experimenting with Torque and Mods of Unreal we realized that a single player first person shooter suits setting and idea much better. The idea is layed out much clearer in a singleplayer, and more people are drawn to play the game. In fact the game has lots of downloads and people still play it. So far there are 365'345 corpses amassed into a "Leichenberg". Laichenberg is a play of words: mountain of spawns instead of mountain of corpses. The game counts all frags and registers all their locations on a world map. Laichenberg therefore also shows who plays this game and how people play it. At present the USA is in the lead with 136'515 deads, followed by Germany with 29'110 deads and Canada with 18'918 deads. The final scene of the game by the way shows you the disposal of the latest frags or corpses in a refuse incineration plant.

With your latest work, "Discrimination Pong" you subverted a classic arcade game to comment on racism. How can videogames change society or, at least, make us aware of inequality and abuse?

- Videogames are modern fairy-tales. They allow the player to feel important and provide her or him with the idea to live a successful life. This way they may help a person through his everyday life and doing so they help to preserve our society. If you include discrimination into a two player rivalry game like Pong, you might realize how unfair discrimination is in our world. Games make the world experiencable, comprehensible and replicable. But at the same time there are more and more games that make the player pay money in order to reach next levels or receive powerful in-game artefacts. Games are door openers for all sorts of ideas we don't like in games, but at the same time we try adopt them in a playful mode and point them out.

How do you think videogames will change our culture and how we experience culture in the future?
- Videogames are like any other modern mass media: You can use them positively or abuse them. You can use them to be critical with society and media, but you can also use them as a tranquilizer or sleep inducing drug. Games are ideal as sleep inducing drugs, they calm you down and at the same time they propel you. This is how many videogames (even first person shooter) transport the most important values of the western world like competition, rivalry, labour, consumption and career. More and more the world itself seems to become a videogame (not just at the stock exchanges) and we have to ask ourselves: "If everyone is playing - who does actually play?"

How would you describe the Game Art scene in Switzerland?
- Actually there are not too many Game Art groups in Switzerland. There is the native artgroup "Mobiles Kino" that develops analogue game machines with movie projectors and "NotSONoisy" that re-enacts Space Invaders and Pac Man with human beings in movie theatres. And some years ago the game artists Margarete Jahrmann and Max Moswitzer moved from Vienna to Switzerland. They are known for their projects "Nybble Engine" and "Ludic Society". We hope that besides all of them there is an unknown quantity of yet silent game artists that produces Game Art.

The interview took place in February 2011.

Rewell Altunaga: Game Art in Cuba

Rewell Altunaga (b. 1977, Camagüey) is a Cuban artist and curator, living and working in Havana. In 2002, Altunaga graduated from the Academia de Artes Plásticas Oscar Fernández Morera, Trinidad, Cuba where he studied painting, ceramics and photography and become fascinated by the potential of new media - especially video games - as platforms for artistic expression. In the past decade, Altunaga has produced a significant number of machinima, mods, and other kinds of works based on videogames.

When did you become interested in videogames? What specific titles or genres did you find especially fascinating, and why?
-In the early 1990s, the Socialist block collapsed and Eastern Europe remained sharply divided - a series of local conflicts and "settling of accounts" dominated the first part of the decade. This major historical event had been somehow prefigured by the nuclear accident of Chernobyl in 1986 and by the retreat of the Soviet troops from Afghanistan in 1988. As a kid, unaware or uninterested about the small and big dramas that were occupying the minds of the so-called grown-ups, I spent my time playing videogames with my peers. We were eventually hired to play games professionally in underground circuits and we were happy to make extra money on top of our "official" salaries. An entire generation of Cubans grew up in the small worlds of Mario, Contra, Duke, Doom, Quake and other games. We experienced the 8, 16 and 32-bit generation, waging childish revolutions to save false princesses and illusory societies; while our confused generational parents – maddened by the disintegration of their nourishing power – had exhausted the "programmed answers" about Good and Evil. Moreover, their dream of "overthrowing" a bigger enemy had vanished and their conflict appeared to us even more remote and "virtual". Today – between irreconcilable diasporas and incoherent professions – the "blessed children" are scattered throughout the world. Nowadays, my passion for commercial videogames is minimal, and it only applies to specific titles. I find myself attracted by the symbolical relief offered by a satirical parody like GTA, the controversial and

paradoxical sandbox game whose new edition ignites an anti-ethical debate among a few political intriguers and intellectuals who seem to be more concerned with the irreverent programmed dis-order of Rockstar cities than the real and wild madness of humankind. I also love the subjectivity of some FPS that are trivially based on current conflicts; they allow the user to perceive simultaneously the impulses of death and destruction that underlie the super-structure, the market, and the consumption of current conflicts.

In the past, you have produced a series of video game mods and machinima. For instance, Coward (2007) is based on Delta Force: Black Hawk Down + Team Sabre (2006). Ammu-nation (2006) is a mod of Grand Theft Auto: Vice City (2002). The Journey (2009) is both a mod and machinima based on Grand Theft Auto. Why are you so fascinated by this medium? Why did you choose games to make art, especially machinima?
- In my artistic practice I have always tried to create sudden breaks in the space and time continuum by creating specific links between the "real" and virtual worlds. The unlimited exchange of resources between the different "places" of illusion provides priceless inspiration. My work is based on an appropriation of the variables that constantly determine the search on different levels of "realities" – as such, video games may be understood as one of these levels– of the nature of what I experience in art as "source" of pure experience, immediate contact with reality. An attitude of apprehension as exercise of a "non-belief" or total negation. This strategy of localization of phases of mental alienation enables me to simultaneously escape and dismantle the control structures that rule and constrain social conscience. The objects and phenomena then all become a new perceptual material.

How would you describe the Cuban Game Art scene? Are there many Cuban artists using videogames as their main inspiration to create art?
- Very few artists have approached this area. Therefore, I would not say that there is a blossoming Game Art scene in Cuba. The fact that a gamer may become an "artist" or that an artist – in most cases, a

casual player– comes across, incidentally, with game aesthetics and coding, are very different experiences and attitudes with regard to video games, to everyday life as well as art itself. There are few remarkable exceptions, however. Rodolfo Peraza, for instance, uses video games as method to create art, while Jairo Gutiérrez and Fernando Gutiérrez have explored games in a couple of works.

Just like the Internet, the video game culture in Cuba is developing in an underground atmosphere, somehow removed from the broader discourse; it can be said that the creative impulse of the initiators of Net Art –who approached the web as artistic support because it was an easy and economic access in a society in full post-communist crisis– in our case is the other way around. After two decades we find ourselves in a context of disconnection and new-media vigilance, which makes our work have an anti-establishment character in the face of the local power and control mechanisms, but also in the face of the world macro power. In Cuba, Internet is perceived as an illusion, a black world accessible illegally, and strictly linked to piracy – through proxi – the black market or hour quotas that represent more than half the average monthly salary of a common worker. Thus, it can be said that we participate in a process of double alienation, since every illusion is, in turn, alienating.

In this context, there are no official platforms to boost the development of video games; both in the creation and distribution, their production is practically null. The retrogressive dissemination and teaching media still stigmatize it as a form of capitalist alienation. It is still individual persons with small pirate businesses who supply consoles, games and information to a wide range of "home" players. The great paradox lies in the speed with which you may obtain a title after its launching. In a context of absolute control, is it perhaps the same persons who filter private information in the main national servers the ones who download and distribute thousands of gigabytes of movies, documentaries, series, software and video games perfectly organized in weekly entertainment packages delivered to the house doors? Does the system allow this smuggling of information as relief to the ludic abandonment reigning in society, or is it not conscious of it?

Even so, it cannot be said that the videogame moves in an illegal environment, because my country is the paradise of piracy, ideal for the art of "appropriation"; high accuracy licentiousness if you take into consideration that we form a genuine retro "social network". Temporary loop that repeats the subtraction between colonizers and colonized, between conquerors and conquered. Fertile land for cultural studies of the "offline" societies of the 21st century.

You are currently co-curating with Liz Munsell an exhibition called Cuban Virtualities which opens September 5 2013 at Tufts University. What was the main idea behind this exhibition? Is Cuban Game Game Art represented?
- Under the direction of María Magdalena Campos-Pons, a breach of exchange and possibilities opened for artistic practices of performance, relational, process or intervention variables, and with it, for Game Art and Net Art, fearfully avoided by the system of art institutions in Cuba; a system that should reconsider its effectiveness in the face of the circulation speed of activity in the 21st century, of the –ever greater– involved knowledge that mobilizes the artistic experience and in the face of an independent art market.

Cuban Virtualities emerged as the result of the work performed by Magda (FeFa) during the Eleventh Havana Biennial, a gesture that "corrodes" the old iron curtain that still floats above us, allowing collaboration links, the possibility of accomplishment for this project and others. In that curatorial work Liz and I had no specific interest on Game Art, and that is why only Rodolfo takes part with works in this genre. One can say that this exhibition is an attempt to revert the creative isolation from a context in which, sadly, art has been dosed as mere practice of economic survival. Typical error of territories where the human being has been reduced to a mass of frustrated wishes of individual opulence. A bug in the practice of egalitarianism.

Here we are presenting a new generation of Cuban artists the majority of whom, although unknown in the international context, occupy a key zone in the Island's present symbolic production. We are not speaking of textures, forms or volumes of painting and sculpture; we are talking mainly of works, the majority of which were thought for the Internet by artists of a country where this service has been censured and replaced by a caricature officially known as "intranet".

Practicing inverse engineering, dismantling, de-compiling, recycling, hacking, cracking, modifying, deconstructing, disarming or pirating technology is a practice that should not be judged when speaking of artistic purposes. We are not interested in a specific object as merchandise, but as symbol. We do not work creating entities; we face a contextualization process of territories in the surrounding reality. We appropriate fragments of different zones of the stage-situation of the present individual to give you back a symbolical, philosophical or poetical product that dialogues about common problems of these two societies facing each other and the rest of the world. To allow the "accident" that affects every kind of technology —according to Paul Virilio— is to allow its development and to civilize the technique. Beyond our rusty historical walls, we are interested in the reflection on the human being in contemporary times and the role that technology plays in it.

The interview took place in June 2013.

Chris Clarke: Game Art in Irland

Chris Clarke is curator at Lewis Glucksman Gallery. In March 2012, Clarke was involved in Game On, a massive event that feature artworks based on desktop interfaces, video games and online software. Among the participating artists were Peggy Ahwesh (US), Paul B. Davis (US), Michael Bell-Smith (US), Cao Fei (CN), Faith Denham (IE), JODI (NL), Oliver Laric (AT), Conor McGarrigle (IE), and Takeshi Murata (US).

What are the main philosophy behind the Lewis Glucksman Gallery? And can you describe the goals of Game On?
- The Lewis Glucksman Gallery is based at University College Cork in Cork, Ireland. It primarily presents curated thematic exhibitions of international and Irish artists, often connected to a certain aspect of different educational disciplines within the university. However, Game On comes out of a recent strand of touring programmes we've developed, beginning with Wishful Thinking, a screening of 16mm films curated by Matt Packer and including Roman Ondak, Jaki Irvine and Luke Fowler amongst others. With Game On, I wanted to produce a similar programme of short films that could be screened with a curatorial introduction to contextualise them within the wider history of hacktivism, gaming and new media art. It is still primarily a film programme, emphasising works that use the language and aesthetics of gaming, online applications, software and social networks. So, for example, Conor McGarrigle's work is a heavily pixelated version of an episode of Mad Men made by downloading the show from a file-sharing network and disrupting it mid-transmission, Conor McGarrigle, MadMEN BitTorrent Edition, 2012 while Peggy Ahwesh and Faith Denham use extant formats of video games (Tomb Raider and Counter-Strike respectively) to subvert the initial narrative or subtext of the original games. In this way, they share the same spirit as hackers in appropriating and reconfiguring these materials.

Where could you see the program during the tour?
- Game On toured to venues across Ireland, including Siamsa Tire, Tralee; 126, Galway; Occupy Space, Limerick; Garter Lane, Waterford; and Source Arts Centre, Thurles, before finishing up back at the Lewis Glucksman Gallery. I introduced and contextualised the programme at each venue and answered questions from audiences afterwards.

Irish artists Faith Denham and Conor McGarrigle took part in Game On. Are they representative of a larger Irish Game Art scene? Are the other artists in Ireland who are experimenting with video games and art?
- Ireland has a small but active gaming scene, albeit one that I'm not heavily involved in. During the series, Thurles was of particular interest as the audience consisted of a number of enthusiastic gamers, who had organised a video game tournament beforehand. It was also quite intriguing to see which works they found most interesting – especially as the group included a number of programmers and IT students. As you mentioned, Game On included works by two Irish artists – Conor McGarrigle and Faith Denham - but I've come across a few others since then and through the programme, who, even if they're not explicitly working with video games, are quite adept with new media and internet art.

What's your own experience and interest in video games?
- My own experience with gaming is fairly limited. I would have played games like Super Mario and Legend of Zeldawhen I was younger but have only recently returned to it through my son (who is always getting me to play Nintendo DS with him!). Saying that, I spent a few years working at Cornerhouse in Manchester prior to moving to Cork and the gallery there had a strong emphasis on new media art, exhibiting artists like Masaki Fujihata, Charles Sandison, Georges Legrady, and Pat O'Neill. I also assisted on new commissioned works by Shaina Anand and Anne-Marie Schleiner while I was there. Plus, in the Northwest of the UK, you had close proximity to a number of other spaces exploring these ideas, such as FACT in Liverpool (who showed JODI and Pipilotti Rist),

Castlefield Gallery (who had showed Cory Arcangel at the time), The Whitworth Gallery (with a retrospective of Lynne Hershmann) and the Abandon Normal Devices festival. So my initiation into gaming and new media really came through contemporary art.

Are you planning any future program or exhibitions with video games and art?
- For the moment, I have no gaming-related projects in the pipeline but certainly have my eyes open for other projects in this field. There is an audience – only in 2009 did Belfast host the ISEA conference and a huge audience of new media artists and programmers came out of nowhere for it – but it remains to be seen whether Ireland will become the next big site for such work.

The interview took place in March 2012.

Johan Löfgren: Game Art in Sweden

Johan Löfgren is a Swedish artist who has been experimenting with videogames for the past ten years. Born in 1972, Löfgren has created eclectic works such as "from bits to pieces" (2002-2007) and "neo-arcade" (2008), which remediate the retro-aesthetic of pixel art and early computers/consoles.

Several artists who experimented with videogames, like yourself, were born in the 1970s, and belong to what has been called "the videogame generation". In that decade, videogames "invaded" the media landscape – actually, they create brand new landscape, a new visual language, a new form of art. What did you find remarkable in this medium, so remarkable that you decided to use it to create art?
-Recently I visited the national portrait gallery at Gripsholm Castle and took the guided tour, when the guide announced: -And there we have Richard III of England!
-It's impossible he is so still and 2-dimensional almost flat, it must be a painting, I stated.
In our culture we see a painted portrait as a true representation of a historical person and we have learned over the centuries to accept paintings as a proxy of reality. Those who grew up in late '70s and mid '80s consumed vast amount of abstract iconic graphics playing Atari 2600 games like Space Invaders or arcade games like Asteroids. We accepted a vectorised triangle as a spaceship or a yellow circle with a pizza slice missing as "Pac-Man". When I began to create paintings I used Dan Silva's DeLuxPaint back in the early '80s and I'm still using software to develop my ideas and content -it has become my crayons.

The pixel is the quintessential element in your artistic production. What do you find so fascinating about pixels?
- In a philosophical sense, I am breaking down the view into smaller but more visual pieces. However I think of it as creating something from scratch. My work is about "constructing", as in the opposite of "de-constructing". Sampling retro video games has never been my

thing... The area of photoreceptors in the back of my eyes is to hardly etch by it and the cerebral cortex too damaged. I like to connect different thought and content from the past and visions of the future in my work.

What was the rationale behind "Sketchbook of the Neo-arcade"?
-Neo-Arcade gave me the chance to revisit monochrome marble statues in a novel way. I basically repainted them. Reconnecting with the addictive light that flooded my eyes in the video-arcades. And the layers of meaning in the word Arcade was igniting my imagination to me when I was recording my own screen drawings. A pixel journal of what happened when the multi-colored lines sprouted out over the surface, a moving option for the final still-frame.

Is there any differences between creating a picture on a computer screen or on a canvas?
-Not really, it sprung out of the same source -just reflecting the ideas of the Big Brush in the sky ;) My analog paintings were heavily inspired by my digital works in the sense of looks and finish but in the going back and fourth between the disciplines I have strived to make my analog painting more "human" and the digital more machinelike. It's no longer a problem for me to discover a hair from the brush in the dried paint on the squared-out canvas. I now accept that it is a different environment.

What is the meaning of your color palette?
- When I grew up additive colours coming from small lamps in the screen was to me more appealing to me than the sunlight. A painting and its depending on a light source is not that appealing to me. The first time I CMYKed my RGB pics I was devastated of the loss in colour range/depth. I felt that after the printing press was done it was not much left of the original energy.
Any work by Shigeru Miyamoto, "the father of modern video games," has inspired me greatly, color-wise. And John F. Simon, JR. and his work with LCD-panels is work that my mind comes coming back.

How would you define the current status of Game Art in Sweden?
-It has struck me as odd since my days in art school to know that the majority of the painters felt more connected to the work of Caravaggio or Piero della Francesca than the work of, let's say, companies like Namco or Nintendo. I understand the fascination of the unique mark of the human hand and the total massive imprint that the nature can have for a creative mind. I'm as well inspired by the "calligraphy of the hand". But to turn away from the screen in these days and say it's not a medium of content or a carrier of the human thought that's to me highly remarkable.

The interview took place in April 2010.

Olle Essvik: Game Art in Sweden

Since childhood, artist Swedish artist Olle Essvik has been interested in video games as an artistic medium, especially old Macintosh games. In his artist statement, produced in 2005, Essvik reveals his fascination for interactive media via a Flash video. In his latest works, "Waiting For" and "Endgame", Essvik adapted & updated Samuel Beckett for the digital age. The former is described by the artist as "A theatrical play with a number of set instructions constantly repeated, but each time in a different order. The piece consists of a programmed and interactive animation sequence shown online and resembling a computer game, but where the concept has been expanded and the actual game element have been left out". The latter, "Endgame", will be released soon.

When did you first encounter videogames? What kind of ludic experiences inspire/d you as an artist?

- Videogames have always been part of my life, and I can't remember a time when they weren't. As very young I remember playing games on GameWatch, Nintendo consoles, and later Atari and the Commodore 64. I remember as a kid wishing for an Amiga, but I never got one. My parents owned a Macintosh and the supply of games was limited and expensive.

In these new games that I have constructed, the graphics are inspired by the old Mac games I played as a kid, created in MacPaint. As I grew up and became interested in other things, the gaming gradually disappeared. I think most of my friends also stopped playing, and maybe it wasn't until the arrival of the Internet and games like Quake that I started to get interested again. But this renewed interest was rather short-lived. I soon realised that I would get caught up in it and spend a lot of time on something that I in fact considered rather meaningless and unproductive, however entertaining. I didn't find enough compelling meaning or narrative in the games, so I decided to quit playing and spend my time on other things. It makes me sound overly self-disciplined and boring, but I have never regretted it. These days, my gaming is very limited.

I am inspired by the simple games that I remember from my childhood. Every now and then I check out the games being made today, primarily indie-games and Game Art.
I don't consider myself a game designer in the traditional sense of the word. My primary sources of inspiration are literature and art. It is not the traditional elements of the game that interest me, but rather the narratives of games and the new possibilities for telling a story in non-linear and interactive way.

One of you first games is called "Broken Narratives (207)", which you described as a "collection of games/narratives. Games without levels, win/lose thinking, games without purpose, just narratives with the structure and navigation of a computer game". It seems to me that you are fascinated by the game medium and by the videogame aesthetics, but at the same time, your artistic performance consists in emulating this ludic aspects rather than using gameplay as an expressive means. In a sense, you've removed the gamesness from the games. This work, in particular, has a tangible/concrete nature: you udeveloped a portable sculpture that can be played with a joystick...
- Yes. I constructed that game around 2006. It consists of a number of narratives tied together. The game isn't very conceptual, but rather a visual experience. It can be compared to a dream in which you can walk around, and it contains several references to the games I used to play as a child. Both the sounds and the characters can be found in games or in memories of games that I owned in my childhood.
The title "Broken narratives" refers to a narrative that has been taken apart, broken up, fragmented, like in memories or dreams. The process of creating that game gave birth to further thoughts and ideas on the possibilities of using video games for constructing non-linear narratives without beginning or end. The game has also been exhibited in a gallery context, installed into a module built from old pieces of furniture from my childhood. A kind of strange, portable arcade game constructed as a suitcase. So, besides being

available on the Net, the game was also a sculpture and a physical art-piece.

This Winter you are introducing two new art games inspired by Samuel Beckett's plays,"Waiting for Godot" and "Endgame". What is your relationship to Beckett? What is the rationale behind this original combination of theatre and videogames?
- My relationship to Beckett consists in having seen and read some of his plays. I got the idea for the game while watching "Waiting for Godot" and getting inspired by the elements of repetition in the play, where the second act is basically a repetition of the first. (In the plot, the two main characters, Vladimir and Estragon are sitting around waiting for a man named Godot. The first and second act are essentially the same, in the sense that they both consist of the main characters waiting for Godot, and that in essence nothing happens.) The concept can be seen as a metaphor for our human existence with its every day repetitions, but also for computer games and the loop of computer programming. I saw the possibility for constructing a repeating narrative that was always essentially the same, but with small alterations and new events. Similar to "Waiting for Godot", but with an unlimited number of acts. The second game, "Endgame", has borrowed its title from another Becket play, but apart from that there are few references to the actual play.

I am an admirer of Beckett and the spirit of the times in which he lived and worked. Waiting for Godot was released in 1952 in postwar Paris. A time characterized by despair and a general loss of faith in society. A time when Existentialism, Pataphysics, the Theater of the Absurd where important artistic and philosophical movements. Themes like boredom, hopelessness, and emptiness dominated theater, literature and art. There was a specific sense of tragedy and comedy that is very much present in Waiting for Godot. My previous works, like these new ones, have often been dominated by themes like mundanity, despair and emptiness, but always with a sense of humor of absurdity. If that sense of absurdity or tragicomedy were not recognised, my works would be perceived as completely hopeless and tragic. I am interested in the same themes that characterized Beckett's work. Even if the form of this new work resembles that of a computer game I actually think that it has more in common with a theater play. "Endgame" is violent and dark, but the soundtrack, consisting of 1910s marching music, and the atmosphere is so absurd and exaggerated that only comedy remains. The game will be released later this autumn.

What is "Waiting for" about?
-The game is about mundanity, emptiness and the repetition of every day existence. We wander through the repetitions of our every day life waiting for something else to happen. The programming of my game contains a large archive of objects and events. These objects and events are then selected, partly randomly and partly as a result of conscious or unconscious interaction, which combines to change what the game will look like.

The constants of the game are the beginning and end, which are always the same. Nothing happens, and yet everything happens. The game will never repeat itself completely, even if you might experience it as a repetition, as the same thing. My game consists of an eternal number of acts and has no precise beginning or end, even though they remain the same. The second game is linear and has a more precise meaning, but it becomes a non-meaning since it provides an answer where there actually is none.

Your practices include curatorial work. For instance, in 2008 you curated the seminal exhibition "My Computer" in Gotemborg. The event focused on computer based art and art games. Scandinavia - and Sweden in particular - seems to be a fertile ground for some of the most original and creative examples of Game Art. What is your take about the Swedish Game Art scene? More importantly... Is it a "scene"?
- I know of very few people working with games. Most of the people I know of from before are not very active today. Perhaps the scene has found different forms with new players. Though I must confess that I am not sure exactly where the concept ends. I have had works, which curators have labelled game-art just because they

contain programming, but which I myself have seen as something completely different.

If game-art is defined as art in the form of games or containing references to games, my feeling is that not alot is being made in Sweden today. Some people I know who used to be active have moved in other directions. But since not much is written and since I know so few people who are active, it is obviously very difficult to be aware of everything that is happening, so I might have missed something.

That is why it is extremely important for us who work with game-art that there is someone who writes about it, since the traditional art media show relatively little interest. When an art form is unknown or not trendy it very easily happens that people abandon it for other art forms that get more attention.

The interview took place in November 2011.

Shinji Murakam: Game Art in Japan

When the video game industry in USA crashed in 1983 it was the beginning of the golden age for the Japanese videogames with companies as Nintendo and Sega. Top stars game designer as Shigeru Miyamoto, created during this period legendary videogames as Super Mario, Donkey Kong and The Legend of Zelda. The RGP genre took a big jump when Hironobu Sakaguchi presented the successful RPG series Final Fantasy in 1987. With such a historical background you would think that Japan, as USA and Europe, have a strong tradition with contemporary artists inspired by videogames and that you would find regular exhibitions with Game Art in the country. After all Japan is the promised land of popular culture. But surprisingly it is very quiet from the Japanese Game Art scene. An exception is the Japanese artist Shinji Murakami, who was born in 1980 in Osaka and grew up, as he self describes it on a healthy diet of 8-bit computer games, with The Legend of Zelda as a favourite.

On you homepage you say that you was "raised on a healthy diet of classic 8-bit video games". What are so fascinating with 8-bit graphic and what kind of games inspires you?
-I love the simple expressions, and minimalism in the games. Other important thing is the nostalgia, because I was crazy about Nintendo (NES and Super NES) when I was a kid. I think it's amazing that Nintendo's famous 8-bit characters could express so much with only 16×16 pixels! And how they created these very large worlds with recycling limited materials in each game is also fascinating. The kind of game that inspires me most is role-playing game and side-view action game, especially role-playing game like the first Zelda.

You started as a street artist and used to tag cities with your 8-bit charactersBoco and Kid Snz. Can you tell me something about these characters?
- Yes, I started as a street artist, by putting stones in the streets which I painted and tagged. I couldn't tag on the walls at first, because I was very afraid of being arrested. I don't like the writers

who tag the names that sound like English, I mean most Japanese can't speak English well. A also felt a sense of incongruity in working with the European or American style. So I began tagging the image of the sword and the shield, those images are inspired from stereotype items of RPG. Next I drew a lot of characters to find my favourites ones as my new tags. A girl friend of mine chooses a special one from those characters. I obeyed her choice, because I believe in the intuition of the girl, because the character "Kawaii" (means cute in Japanese). That's the original Boco. Boco's concept is a simple drawing which looks likes a kid's drawing. It means kid's drawing with a minimum expression of drawing like 8-bit graphic is a minimum of a bitmap image. And I think that Kid Snz expresses most of minimum bitmap graphic by only 9×7 pixels.

What do you think about street art as an illegal act?
- My opinion about street art is contradiction. Did you see my street work that bombed the billboard? I put the logo of NIKE or NISSAN on the same place with my drawing. In this case, I tried an experiment that people will recognize those billboards show true advertisement by putting a logo. One more thing, though it is an illegal act, but some gallery owners such as Jeffrey Deitch very like it, and a market is formed. I just think that the scenery on the street is going to be unimaginative if street art disappears.

In a series called RPG you have worked with maps, for example you have created a map over Central Park in New York in Final Quest 1 style? Can you tell me how this RGP maps are created and why you choose to work with a style that reminisces about an old Japanese art style which uses stamps on wooden panel?
-"If I made a tree icon and put a lot of them next to each other, I'd be able to make a forest map!" This was the little light bulb of an idea that started my map artwork in 2003. I put my original stamps with images of "Map data" and "Item data" on the wood panel which had a white painted background. The "Character data" I draw with a marker. I used to make only small works, because the rooms are small in Japan. So the stamp was matched for the method to repeat the image for that size. The surface of the canvas had small

irregularities, so I use the wood panel that is more flat than canvas. I am not conscious that my work could remind of a particularly Japanese old style. In fact, after I moved to New York, I used silk-screening to make bigger sizes.

In your latest work you have started to explore 3D-8bit? What was it that made you go from 2D to 3D?
- Yes, I am trying to explore the art of 3D-8bit. In Japan in 2005, there was a joint marketing campaign between Pepsi and Nintendo gaining recognition for its production of a 3D-8bit version of Super Mario Bros. Japan has a big Otaku culture today, so a lot of new figures (it means like a toy doll) are always released, but this product excited me and was very inspiring. I always want to discover new styles, and I was interested in making a sculpture in a new style. As an artist that has continued to utilize 8-bit games as a motif in his artwork, I felt compelled to create my own 3D-8bit artwork, and in 2009, I completed Fruits Bowl.

Can you tell me some about the Japanese Game Art scene? Are the many contemporary artists inspired by videogames in Japan today? And are there any interest from art museum and galleries to show this kind of art?
- First there is a necessary thing to explain, unfortunately there is almost no market for contemporary art in Japan today, and there is almost no culture of purchasing art. It is a big reason that I moved to New York. In fact, people in Japan don't understand why the Japanese artist Takashi Murakami is famous in the world, and they are not curious about it. There are a lot of art museums and galleries in Japan, but it seems to be a place for the elderly to entertain themselves. Some galleries collect money from artists to loan their space. Do you think that is attractive art scene with such a situation? Do you believe that there are any critics who have an advanced review? I don't think so. There are a lot of artists who use motif from Manga or Anime in the tradition of Takashi Murakami, but it is rare with video game artist. There is my prejudice to some extent, but I mean the answer to this question is almost: No!

The interview took place in October 2010.

Paul Steen: Game Art in Sweden

Paul Steen, born 1972 in Uppsala, is a Swedish artist an journalist. In his art his make references to classic board games and video games.

You latest work, "Art Assault", is a bold, full-frontal attack on the art establishment. How did you come up with the idea? What does the title mean?
- "Art Assault" is a mod of the open source FPS Assault Cube, set in a caricature of the art world, hence the name. It's about hierarchies and the struggle for power. The levels are all modeled after real life galleries and museums, with textures based on photos I've taken myself at the various spots. The bots are named after the most successful living artists according to artfacts.net. They are parted randomly into the teams Outside and Inside, a picture of social boundaries and the struggle between establishment and wannabes. They even shoot their own team members if they stand in the way. Every time someone falls a new bot spawns in his name: Fame is fickle and there is always someone there to take your place. No one side ever really has the upper hand for long.
I am always looking for materials and means of expression on the one hand that fit different concepts I'm mulling on the other hand, and I thought the way I could edit Assault Cube made it a fitting platform to make a picture of things I wanted to say about the art world.
One thing that fascinates me with the FPS genre in games (Although you find it in other games like RTS) is that you can discern two different tactics for survival described by Gilles Deleuze in A Thousand Plateaus: The sedentary farmer and the nomad who masters mobility. This corresponds to how FPS online players often resort to either "camping" or "ramboing".
I made a somehow similar smaller game several years ago that was gracefully lost in a computer crash before I could show it:Art Counter-Strike. It was a slightly minimalist and cartoonish third person shooter made with Coldstone. "Art Assault" is the realization with better means of many things I wanted to say back then.

The "modded" art-gallery is a recurrent theme in Game Art. The idea of going berserk in a sacred space, devoted to art, is very popular among the enfant terribles experimenting with games. One early example is "Museum Meltdown" by Palle Torsson and Tobias Bernstrup. More recent artworks include Michiel Van Der Zanden's "Museum Killer" (2008) and Chris Reilly's "Everything I Do is Art, But Nothing I Do Makes Any Difference, Part II Or: How I Learned to Stop Worrying and Love the Gallery". Are you familiar with such works? Is "Art Assault" an homage to these previous efforts?

- Palle Torsson is an old acquaintance of mine that I have great respect for, for his entire work, not just his game related stuff. I am familiar with other contemporary artists making use of FPS or games in art and I'm happy to inscribe myself in that context, but my greatest iinspiration has to be the Swedish artist Öyvind Fahlström and his Cold War Monopoly games. His example showed me in the first plac that it was possible to construct simulations or a set of rules and to present them as a work of art, an interpretation of the world, a metaphor.

What lies ahead for "Art Assault"? Will you continue to develop the game in the future, adding extra levels and features? Are you planning new exhibitions?
- In December 2010, I'm showing a live game play projection of "Art Assault" at the opening of #RANK, an alternative event to Art Miami. Jennifer Dalton and William Powhida are organizing talks and showing artists making work related to power and hierarchies in art at the Seven art space. I will surely make more levels for "Art Assault" but not necessarily another FPS. Other games for sure, but I don't feel like I necessarily need to use a computer to make processual art.

You were born in the early Seventies, like the medium of the videogame itself. It is safe to assume that you grew up playing digital games? How did videogames affect you personally, and as an artist?

-Growing up in the '70s and '80s it's clear that arcades and computer games played a big role. I used to play Space Invaders with pebbles and pieces of wood in the forest in Sweden where I grew up. Later I had a Spectrum 48k and made my own crude programs in BASIC long before I went to art academy and learned to paint properly. It was a way of creating your own world. I think that the openness of creating your own rules and modifying them to see what happens, the whole idea of the freedom of play was a lasting experience that I somehow missed later on in the classical form of painting I was taught.

What are your thoughts on the Swedish new media art scene, especially in relation to video game-based interventions?
- I think Sweden has a long and interesting tradition of new media and game art. Sweden has a relatively big games industry which I think is the result of a general openness and curiosity towards new media that has been there for decades. Video games have been referenced in art by many in my generation who may not be known for that in particular. Johan Thurfjell for instance. We have as a country been technologically advanced for a long time and there has been a great openness to new media in the cultural sphere. There has both been an iinfrastructure of available technology, a willingness among many artists to use it, and a political will to encourage it and fund projects. In an art context this might not always be known to the outside world since much of the structures of the art world are still built on face to face meetings, and Sweden simply has an unfortunate geographical placement. It's a schlep. Unfortunate really, because there are some really world class Swedish artists.

The interview took place in December 2010.

Marque Cornblatt: Game Art in USA

Marque Cornblatt lives in San Francisco and calls himself a "Conceptual Technologist". He is exploring "hyper-mediated identity", i.e. the borderline between virtual and real identity, the grey area between being and performing in tangible and online spaces. This concern has become a staple of contemporary Hollywood cinema - think, for instance, of such movies as Gamer (2009), Avatar (2009) and Surrogates (2009). All these movies imagine a future where humans are living through their avatars, and where virtual and real identities are becoming indiscernible. Cornblattt has been investigating the same shifting boundaries through a series a bold artistic interventions. He has also produced a series of ground-breaking performances in game spaces, including "Grand Theft Auto IV Crime Free Law-Abider, A Performance Art Project" (2008).

Your MFA Thesis announces "The Emergence of the MediaSapien". What is the MediaSapien, exactly?

- The MediaSapien is a term I coined to describe the current evolution of the human animal as it becomes a hybrid of flesh and technology. Although the notion of the human/machine cyborg is nothing new, the past few years have seen the exponential growth of human identity as filtered through digital technologies. In a remarkably short span of time, people have begun to spend their time in virtual territory and share their lives on social networks to such an extent, that many people find virtual life to be more fulfilling and engaging than real life.

From the outside it may be easy to dismiss these people as preferring fantasy over reality, the truth is that the territory of interpersonal significance has shifted, and physical proximity has become less important to quality social discourse. Our friends, lovers, co-workers and peer groups are more likely to be geographically dispersed than ever before in human history, yet our ability to engage each other on deep and intimate levels has never been greater.

Can you explain the genesis of your Xbox 360 self-portraits?
- The Xbox portrait series is a body of work made using only commercially available games on the Xbox console - I decided to limit myself to the tools provided within each game without any additional hacking, modding or coding. The reason for this limitation came from earlier self portrait work made within Second Life. In the SL work, I found the high quality and depth of the tools to actually work against my intent, by allowing limitless options during the creative process. It was essentially too easy to make my avatar portrait exactly as I wanted to appear within the virtual space. SL offered no resistance to my presentation as a tall, young, muscular stud. After a few moments of this creative freedom, I ultimately found the work to be like candy. Very appealing but ultimately void of lasting value.

By switching to Xbox games, I found the toolset to be severely limited - only a handful of games offer any kind of character creation tools, and even those are usually limited to game-specific details. For instance, within The Godfather game, it is very difficult to create a character who isn't a mobster, and all the characters in the Tiger Wood's PGA Tour Golf game seem like yuppies, regardless of the effort to look otherwise. This reduced palette actually provided a more interesting environment for creativity by forcing me to work within (and against) the confines of each game while trying to create portraiture that evokes the true nature of the person, as opposed to the archetypes presumed by the game's designers. The resulting portraits seem to reflect everything from Max Headroom to Harry Potter's living paintings to Cindy Sherman's self-portraits.

The self-portrait is a common practice within the history of art. How do videogames and online worlds change/alter this practice? What is the relationship between our identity and our avatar?
- From the earliest cave paintings through modern times, the self portrait has always been a means of establishing one's place in the world - to say "I am here." In this new virtual territory, reputation has become the most important form of social currency, and we are no longer limited to a single identity. For instance, within Facebook

and Twitter, my outward personae is the working artist, on a dating site, I might present myself as younger and richer than in reality. But on Xbox live, I am simply known as a cold-blooded assassin or deadly sniper. Games and virtual territory allow us to have as many identities as we have online communities.

What about Sparky's "Self Portrait Artifact –Roving Chassis I"?
- The Sparky project examines many of the same ideas and issues as my other work but approaches the conversation from a different starting point. Wherein the video and game-based work explores the hybridization of people and technology within virtual territory, the Sparky project investigates the human/machine hybrid in real space.

Originally built in 1994 as an extension of a series of video-based sculptures, Sparky was designed as a free-rolling robot with a video-chat monitor for a head, and the ability to control it from a remote location - essentially providing a remote, real-time, face-to-face chat device. The robot could be set up at a party or event, and the person controlling and appearing on the 'bot's screen could be almost anywhere in the world - The idea was to allow me to attend my own art reception without leaving home. Over the years, Sparky's basic technology has been replaced and upgraded, and now works entire over the Internet using a combination of Skype and custom software. The functionality of Sparky has expanded as well, providing a template for how people may interact in the near future - attending school, visiting museums, or even acting as a "surrogate" in dangerous situations like hostage negotiations.
There are now several start-up's building telepresence robots with a wide range of feature to attempt to define and fill these emerging niches.

When did you interest in videogames as a platform, a means of expression begin, and what do you find interesting or challenging with this medium?
-The first Pong coin-op cocktail table came out when I was six. I have played videogames every day since then. In almost 40 years, games have become slowly (but steadily) integrated into the

collective consciousness, and within the past few years have gained real traction as a serious medium of communication, creativity, education and socializing. Games are now firmly entrenched in the human conversation and have taken their rightful place within the cycle of cultural cause-and-effect alongside film, literature, performance and technology. Videogames have become both inspiration and palette.

The interview took place in September 2010.

Kent Sheely: Game Art in USA

Kent Sheely is a digital artist specializing in New Media, especially in artworks based on the aesthetics and culture of video games. His work is eclectic and electric. Sheely has been experimenting with in-game photography for the last four years and he has produced several game-based installations like Health Station (2009) and Skybox (2008).

In "DoD: A World War II Photo Essay" you play the role of a war photojournalist. As an "embedded" reporter, you both investigate and document a fictional, ludic World War II. Why did you choose this specific event and not, for instance, the current conflicts in Iraq and Afghanistan? What kind of games do you use of your photography projects?
- I had already worked with virtual photography in Grand Theft Auto, and was looking for other ways to explore the concepts I had been thinking about. A lot of multiplayer games are similar in structure, allowing players to choose from a selection of "classes" that focus on different styles of play, but all of these classes are meant to be combat roles; I wondered what would happen if I could subvert this "class" system, and take on a new role (that of a photojournalist) in a live online game, playing war in a new way and breaking the rules a little bit.
I primarily worked with the WWII game Day of Defeat: Source because I was intrigued by its gritty, war-ravaged urban settings and because I wanted my images to pay homage to the photojournalist Robert Capa.

Indeed. Robert Capa, Eddi Adams and Philip Jones Griffiths are some of the most recognized war photographers. How did their work influence your own exploration? What kinds of conclusions did you draw from juxtaposing "real" photographs and "virtual" photographs, as it happens, for instance, in "World War II Redux" (2009)?
- I was ingtrigued by the work of real photojournalists from the World War II era, especially Capa, whose most famous photographs

of the Normandy invasion were infamously blurred and surreal (due to a lab technician's mistake). I liked this aesthetic because of its natural tendency to distort and abstract reality, the figures emerging from the background like ghosts.

In World War II Redux, by deconstructing well-known historical photographs and reenacting them within the confines of the video game technology, my intent was to highlight the loss of meaning that occurs between real historic events and the interpretations of those events we experience through simulation. Despite best efforts to recreate the same imagery and tone from the original, the facsimile always falls short of the mark, but at the same time causes the viewer to see the original with more attention to detail.

The conflict within Day of Defeat is a representation of the battles that actually took place between the Allied and Axis forces in Europe. In creating this new observational role for my character in the game, I wanted to extend the metaphor as far as possible and document the conflict as I experienced it as an outside observer, separating myself from the goals of either team and focusing on capturing the intensity of what was playing out before me. I also wanted the performative nature of the work to stand out in the way I captured the images, with the low camera angles and the doorways framing what my character saw as he peered out from relative safety.

Your photographic documentation of Grand Theft Auto: San Andreas is particularly intriguing. How did you achieve such fascinating results?

- When I started working with Grand Theft Auto, I was already very familiar with the mechanics of other games in the franchise. You, as the player, are presented with a massive environment to explore, and seemingly infinite possibilities. While it seems existential, the game still has a clear set of goals it wants you to accomplish in order to move its primary narrative forward, most of which involve guns, vehicle theft, and copious violence. The idea to "hijack" the game's intent came about while I was playing around with one of the tools in the game, a little camera intended to be used to verify an assassination during one of the game's missions. I found myself abandoning the story altogether, roaming the city and taking photos of the environments, the architecture and the computer-generated citizens going about their business. I tried to emulate my own style of photography as much as possible, framing subjects much as I would in the real world. For me, capturing these images was a record of what I had seen, even if it never really existed.

Pushing further, I started digging through the game's code, removing the aspect of danger from the game, disabling the player's ability to use anything but the camera and turning the player's character into a street photographer. I wanted to transform a game with such heavy cultural baggage into a viable tool for creation and expression, to appropriate the game's universe from a mere backdrop of a violent story into a living subject to be captured and explored through still images.

In your recent series Zappers (2011), you replaced guns in movie stills with images of Nintendo "zapper" light gun controllers. Visually, this pastiche produces hilarious consequences, as the tension of original scene is defused and deflated...

-When I was young, my parents were reluctant to let me watch movies that had scenes of violence, afraid I wouldn't be able to separate them from reality. They would carefully explain, "Those are just actors, and they're pretending to fight each other." "That's just ketchup, it's not real blood." "That monster is just a man in a mask." Around that same time, Nintendo came out with the Zapper controller for the NES that let us simulate the act of shooting things using a controller that actually looked like a gun. We were "acting" as well, mimicking violent acts for the sake of amusement. To me, the Zapper gun represents a state of play, making a game out of something violent and disarming its power to shock and frighten. Combining the two types of images, the film stills and the toy gun, was very funny to me, poking fun at the characters pretending to be threatening and scary.

The interview took place in November 2011.

Wes W. Wilson: Game Art in USA

Wes W. Wilson is an American artist with a MFA from School of the Art Institute of Chicago who works as an artist and web designer (both as practictioneer and as an instructor). In his works, Wilson explores invisible human systems and games that force us to rethink the very notion on "artistic experience". In 2011, Wilson's game "Window Cleaner" was selected by Auriea Harvey & Michaël Samyn aka Tale of Tales to be included in the Notgames Fest in Cologne.

Your game "Window Cleaner" (2010) was featured in the Notgames festival in Cologne, which took place last August. What was your intention behind a game about window-cleaning?
- Well, to begin with "Window Cleaner" is actually the second game I have created with my interest in certain specific kinds of gestural economies, or movements of repetition for maintenance labor. The first game in this series was "Mower" (2009), which I originally made as an art gallery videogame and then later adapted for the iPhone with the help of my friend Jack Stenner.
When I made "Mower", I was living in Florida and Ireland, where there is a lot of lawn space with grass that has to be maintained. There have been times where in my daily commute I'd see people mowing one of the lawns every day. In fact, a lot of neighborhoods give fines of up to hundreds of dollars if they catch you with your front grass too long! Likewise when I moved to Chicago I saw firsthand the people who go up on lifts or belay down ropes to clean the windows. I like these gestures because they never really end. The grass keeps growing and the windows keep getting grimy. And they are very visible.
Although I am also interested in the maintenance of invisible human systems like electricity and waterworks, I don't think I would make a game about that because they require such enormously complex input to regulate and maintain. Plus SimCity has already made a very nice game out of that! I like simple motions. Even though they

maybe aren't very exciting to perform in real life or in my games, they are still very interesting.

In "Air Combat" you created an interactive self-playing modded PlayStation console with the 1995 video game Air Combat, developed by Namco in Japan. While "Mower" and "Window Cleaning" focus on apparently trivial activities, Air Combat is by definition spectacular - very few individuals have ever flew a plane, while almost everybody has some degree of experience with mowing the law and cleaning a window...

- I really love this game. Both the gameplay and the visuals are fantastic, even though they are dated. I've beaten it several times, and I've played some of the sequels. It's a pretty demanding game, and it provides a lot of stimulus with enemies fighting you and ammo, fuel, and your position in the air and over the map to think about. You always pay attention to surviving and completing objectives, but actually the visuals and flying are very beautiful by them self. I used this game because I wanted to make a piece about endless flying, but I was worried about using flight simulators. I have a friend who plays Microsoft Flight Simulator in real time, and picks the longest flights, like New York to Tokyo. All that is needed from the game is to take off and land, and occasionally steer in the middle part during the more than 12 hour flight if you for some reason turn off autopilot. That middle part, the steering and looking around, is all that I used from the original Air Combat game, and I deleted all of the enemies and fuel gauge and music and everything else. The result is just an airplane moving slowly over oceans and continents, with clouds passing by. I also made it so that you can't move up or down so that the viewer can't crash into the ground.

What is the different between the original videogame Air Combat and your installation?

- I could have easily programmed a new flying game from scratch for this installation using the Unity engine, but I chose to hack the existing game Air Combat because the work was not supposed to be about what I created but I removed. In the existing game you play to blow up the bad planes and bomb targets on the ground. This kind of military industrial gameplay is lot of fun and can feel very rewarding for a while because you get constant feedback and information about how well you are doing. But because of the fast pace it is not very thoughtful. My mod leaves just the fighter jet and the world it is in.

A fun side note is that weeks after the show closed I happened to talk to someone who had seen it who claimed that they had played it for almost ten minutes because they had always wanted to play this game when it came out many years ago but even on "easy" mode they still got killed too quickly to really get a feel for flying around!

In "Air Conditioned Tower", an interactive 3D art game, you are able tocreate a somber, almost eerie experience using somber color and geometric shapes.

- I was trying to make a dream space where the player is wandering around a mostly empty office building made of glass which through visuals and audio should feel very cold. There is another portion of that same mod which takes the player out into the desert, which is supposed to feel very hot and dangerous, although both are almost entirely lifeless, with only 2 or 3 living things in each area.

"Air Conditioned Tower" was mostly a Half-Life mod which I made mostly focusing on tone and atmosphere. I made it prior to the Window Cleaner game, and I used Half-Life because I thought that the engine and included assets would work well for creating the kind of dreamlike environment I was going for, and indeed the mod looked very pretty when I was done, both with the desert levels and the glass tower levels.

However, it didn't really feel like a success to me because the controls of Half-Life, which is an FPS, are designed to be amazingly fast so that you can shoot lots of zombies and aliens, and I had trouble getting the limited kind of feel that I was going for. I'm really fascinated with how games limit your input. For example, I think what really made the Wii version ofResident Evil 4 great was how the extremely restrictive controls added to the overall suspense of the game. Games like Canabalt, which only uses one button and yet achieves such a nice feel, amaze me.

What have videogames meant to you as an artists and what kind of videogames inspires you in your work?

- I am actually very interested in the overlap between games and art, with work by art collectives like Blast Theory and artists like Wafaa Bilal. Mainstream games ask for and receive a very high level of time commitment, which can be very enjoyable but disappointing to me when I put down a game after several hours of play and realize that I have nothing important to think about about other than motions my avatar was performing and perhaps what I was killing. On the other hand, art typically has to be rapidly consumable, typically in just a few minutes or even seconds.

My favorite art fits into that short amount of time so much story or concept that it gives me enough interesting things to think about and digest that it takes longer to do so than it took to experience the piece. A lot of indie games are working towards this goal as well, putting a lot of art into a shorter experience. The Portal games from Valve had some of the most amazing characters and atmosphere I've seen in a game. Even a one-liner joke game like You Have To Burn The Rope can be very influential on my art practice.

The interview took place in July 2011.

Benjamin Nuel: Game Art in France

"Born in 1981, graduated of the School of Fine Art of Strasbourg and of the Fresnoy, Benjamin Nuel has developed her artistic work in the field of video and film. It was distributed and exhibited in events like the Locarno Film Festival, the New cinema festival of Montreal and the Rencontres Internationales Paris/Berlin/Madrid. His thinking is currently geared towards forms of non-linear narrative, using real-time 3D and codes video game. He just completed a digital work, hotel. Inspired by the mechanics and aesthetics of the video game war, it rests on springs in the order of fascination, curiosity and frustration in an anti-spectacular. There are, as in the rest of his artistic production, issues of utopia and survival, a certain taste for the drift and the desire to explore areas of friction between the codes and genres. Delineate an area, build a world impossible, sliding between different time" from artist's homepage.

You have been working with both video and machinima. What are the strengths and weaknesses of these two formats?
- Not really. Making a machinima is, of course, easier. An artist still needs to face - and overcome - pragmatic hurdles, but compared to other media, using machinima for making animation is much more approachable. To me, creating a machinima and shooting a video are not essentially dissimilar. What changes is the shooting technique. In-game animation can be hard to predict. It's hard to plan events and situations whereas in film, the director is almost like God. Machinima is a good trade off, a reasonable compromise between a film and a videogame. It lies at the intersection between thee two media. I love creating a film by simply manipulating my mouse.

Who are your favorite film & machinima directors? Who influenced - directly or indirectly - your artistic interventions?
-Honestly, I'm not a true connoisseur of machinima, but the work of someone like Eddo Stern is full of meaning for me. Machinima - and generally real-time and low-poly - are attractive if one is interested in mixing fiction and sculpture, the kinds of arts where I believe the

most interesting things are now taking place in contemporary art. As for cinema, I am amazed by classic works of great directors. Even if they did not inspire me directly, Clint Eastwood and David Cronenberg fascinate me. I am specifically thinking about Cronenberg's approach to cinema - he went from the plastic, organic, around the monstrosity of his early films up to Crash and eXistenZ, to a new aesthetics where the original elements are still present, but in subtler, less explicit ways. Finally, I would love to make a great love story like Two Lovers by James Gray.

When did your interest for videogames as an artistic medium begin? What kind of games do you prefer to work with, and why?
- Silent Hill 2 sparked my interest for the medium. This is not a conventional game. Rather it is an open text, that is, open to interpretation. The explicit goals, like puzzles and riddles, are not very interesting per se. Nevertheless, Silent Hill 2 allows the player to experiment freely within a very peculiar space. Its overabundance of options runs through the entire experience, actually, it defines the experience itself. The slow pace of the game, which could ruin the enjoyment in another context or genre, here becomes its very essence. Wandering through a deserted, eerie town, walking on desolated sets, the cumbersome fights (something that I'd rather avoid tout court)... And yet, these liminal, interstitial moments, are more important that the so-called main narrative. The game destabilizes you... The geographical shift, the temporality of the interaction (even if SH as a linear structure after all, you can find yourself stuck for a while in a spot, and this condition affects your psyche, your mood), the physical confrontation with the world... To me Silent Hill 2 is closer to a sculpture than to a horror film... Its plasticity, its materiality, its architecture is unlike that of film - and most games, for that matter.
Oh, I forgot an important moment in my history of video game: Daggerfall. The playable space was so vast, gosh, I remember the land, the dungeons ... But also the bugs, the glitches, many flaws... So many times I found myself passing through the walls of the dungeons, "discovering" hidden areas across this dark matter,

the void. I remember feeling dizzy. Yeah, I think that feeling led me to create "Hotel".

Ok, let's talk about "Hotel", a machinima that chronicles the struggle between a group of terrorists and a counter-terrorist organization. And yet, there is no violence or "conventional" Hollywood-style action, the same action that most videogames are emulating...
-"Hotel" is a three-part project. The first is a kind of videogame. Indeed, terrorists and counter terrorists are isolated in a luxury hotel in the countryside. But no battles are being fought. It's like a time-out in basketball... Neither violence nor action are taking place. It's how I recreated, re-interpreted the "dead" moments of Silent Hill... The idea came from waiting times in Counter-Strike's games. Once dead, the player can be in a very free browse mode in the level where he was just fighting. It controls a camera that goes very fast in all directions. It passes through the walls to literally leave the world and see it from afar, surrounded by a black nothingness, called the void. This can be done in "Hotel". This gives an ambiguous place to the player who also has the opportunity to assist the daily routine of occupants.

The player will be expected to observe (and disturb) them and try to learn more about this waiting area. According to one's position, one can affirm: "this exists, I can see it, I can even bang against it" or "I reckon they haven't had enough time to finish the piece because it's all gone to pot", and so pass from one to the other. This work is based on springs in the order of the fascination, curiosity and frustration. Inspired by the mechanics of video game war, he proposed a world anti-dramatic. It is finally an object film where the choice of temporality and the strolling to its importance. However, the player must begin the experiment with this question in mind: what is the purpose? And if there is no progress or development of the universe during the experiment (this is a stopped time, in loop) there is a evolution during geographical shift in aware that the player has of his place. It is a story about cohabitation on several levels. The players are located at the points where antagonistic forms clash in an unstable universe. The second part is a feuilleton in ten episodes that takes the opposite course of the video game. We are no more in a stopped time and even if the emptiness of the existence of these characters is still here, they are placed in front of the progressive collapse of their world.

"Pattern Island", a machinima created inside Second Life, is celebrating the "end" of Linden Lab's virtual world. Was that your goal? And how is Second Life "finished" - technically, socially, culturally or even artistically?
- Second Life runs on the individual, he is the center of the world. Yet his presence is only done in the social network, to communicate, or simply to show his avatar or its construction. This duality individual/community was my starting point. Pattern Island combines a form mimicking the classic movie (historic and popular) to capture a collective performance. It is an epic with his hero. The performance captured the collective hip-hop as a manifestation of the ego within a group. The film derives from one form to another. Second Life virtual world as a whole, has a strong link with the utopia and an utopia which becomes reality disappears. For the pioneers, SL was primarily a mental space. Then the population has changed from builders to consumers. The film opens with a opposite situation of expansion known as SL. It's the end of a world, he continuously reduced to a simple reason, the servers that host plots of land close. A monstrous thing goes through the film. It's a kind of Godzilla composed of an aggregate of standard 3D models. It was like a tribute to the builders mixed with concern about how the world goes, the virtual world as the real...

The interview took place in September 2010.

Paolo Pedercini: Game Art in Italy

Born 1981 in Italy, Paolo Pedercini is today a well known artist and game designer. In 1993, he founded Molleindustria, a collective of artists and game designers whose aim is to create "radical games against the dictatorship of entertainment". In the last eight years, Molleindustria has produced an impressive number of highly controversial Flash-based titles such as Oiligarchy, McDonald's Videogame, The Free Culture Game, Operation: Pedopriest, and Phone Story, which was recently banned from the Apple App Store. All these games are example of culture jamming that use videogames as means of expression.

Italy's reputation in the videogame industry is not exactly strong. On the other hand, the Belpaese has produced a remarkable number of groundbreaking artists who use digital games as their medium of choice. How do you explain this apparent paradox?
- It makes some sense: in other contexts some of these artists may have been absorbed by the industry. But since the local game industry is small and marginal, these individuals found other ways to engage with games, either by developing independently (see the critically acclaimed Fotonica by Santa Ragione) or by making game-related art. Another more practical reason is that in Italy there is a small but active group of critics and curators that are passionate about game art. They invested quite a lot of energy in producing events, festivals and publications. That's pretty much what it takes to create a "scene".

Games like "Every Day The Same Dream" and "Inside A Dead Skyscraper" have more existentialist subtexts than more overtly political titles of the recent past. Are you using videogames as a tool to reflect upon the meaning of life? Is this what it takes for games to be accepte as a "true form of art", whatever that means? Would it take a Game Artsuperstar - a 21st century Andy Warhol with a joypad, so to speak - to make it finally happen?
- Tackling supposedly deep themes is in no way a pre-requisite for reaching the status of "high art". You mention Warhol, which is

the perfect example of an artist who didn't (overtly) speak to the human condition. He became extremely relevant by doing the opposite, by embracing the aesthetic and the shallowness of Western consumer culture. Besides, pretty much every attempt to address themes like "the meaning of life" is doomed to fail. It's a very backward, pseudo-universalistic way of thinking about the function of art that somehow persists outside the art circles.

It's true, "Every day the same dream" and "Inside dead Skyscraper" have existentialist overtones but what makes them different from my previous games is just a more emotional, maybe narrative, approach. The theme of workers' alienation or the tension between agency and disempowerment are present in most of my previous, more satirical, games. The truth is that I've been interested in games-as-systems and in the possibilities of messing with games' language for a while, right know I want to try different modes of expression.

You are currently teaching game design and Game Art at Carnegie Mellon University. From your vantage point, what do you think will be next development in Game Art? What are your students mostly interested in nowadays? Augmented reality, smartphone apps, retro games?

- When I hear the term "game art" I think about a) the production of assets in commercial game development and b) the variety of game-inspired or game-related fine art. The latter kinds of art rarely assume a game form; it generally employs established and gallery-friendly formats such as sculpture/installation, video, digital print, painting and so on. It's basically a branch of pop-art that manipulates images and icons taken from the mainstream game culture. While there are a handful of interesting works, it's overall a faddish epiphenomenon of the declining post-modern art. I don't really cover that in my course.

The class is basically about making games starting from artistic perspectives and sensibilities - pretty much in the same way video-artists approached video or net.artists approached the Internet. I'm sure all the emerging technologies you mention will be promptly adopted and dissected by media artists, but if I had to make a more general prediction, I'd first consider that we are facing decades of economic decline and major cuts to art funding. Of course, a fine art market for the ruling class will continue to exists - these people accumulated an immense amount of wealth while wrecking the global economy - but besides the an elite of (mostly deceased) art super stars, the majority of trained artists will be unable to survive by doing what they studied. In a way, it's already like this, but things will get tougher.

So what I foresee is a convergence with the creative industries and more hybrid figures of artists-entrepreneurs. In the context of artistic games I picture more artists competing in the proper game market. Which is not necessarily bad, we may just end up having emptier galleries and better games.

Unlike other game designers, you do not charge a single penny for your work. In fact, most of your titles - aside from Phone Story - are distributed for free on the net. Why did you choose this policy? Is there any market for art games, and are there any collectors, galleries or museums actively buying your games?

- There is room for independent, artistic games in the digital download market. Jason Rohrer's Sleep is Deathwas a commercial success despite the fact it's an insanely odd and inaccessible work. But I'd rather not have this kind of pressure as long as I have other ways to make a living. Also, I wouldn't have nearly as many players if these games were not freely available. I suspect the day a collector offers me to buy one of my games, will be the day I'll decide the project Molleindustria have exhausted all of its potential. And I'll be ready to move on to something else.

The interview took place in August 2011.

Georgie Roxby Smith: Game Art in Australia

"Georgie Roxby Smith is an Australian visual artist working across a range of disciplines exploring new pathways between virtual and physical worlds. Employing a variety of tools - including 3D graphics, live performance, shared virtual spaces, installation and projection - these works explore the increasingly blurred border between materiality, reality, virtuality and fantasy in contemporary culture. Georgie received a Bachelor of Media Arts from Deakin University in 2004. Her graduate studies include a Master of Fine Arts (by Research) with First Class Honours, Post Graduate Diploma in Visual Arts and Master of Visual Arts (by Coursework) from the Victorian College of the Arts, University of Melbourne." (from the Artist's website)

Your MFA thesis, Art 2.0: Identity, Role Play and Performance in Virtual Worlds investigate the ontological and performative overlap between the real and the virtual. What did you discover at the end of your investigation?

- Art 2.0 – Identity, Role Play and Performance in Virtual Worlds was a studio-based research project positioned within the virtual world of Second Life. Focusing on identity as a key provocation, the thesis explored new possibilities of virtual reality software in contemporary art through repositioning "in world" performances into physical installations to create mixed reality video and installations. My initial objectives were to question the idea of materiality through the creation of objects and situations of indistinct form and reality, to explore the position of audience by creating a space where viewers were in multiple realities at once and to break with traditional forms of visual arts practice (installation, new media art, video art and performance) by bringing them together in one "event". By extracting and re-injecting my Second Life avatar into physical space, the work existed on a kaleidoscope of planes: in world, within a body of physical sculptures, as ephemeral projections in space; and as recreated performances by both humans and avatars.

My 2010 work Reality Bytes attempted to bring these multiple realities together by allowing gallery visitors to experience reality cross-overs in all elements of the installation – whether in objects within the room or the way they could access the work, through virtual reality, a physical reality or both simultaneously. The more I worked with Second Life, however, the more it became apparent that this work centred around identity. After two years of reworking, including a residency at Robert Wilson's Watermill Center in New York, the work re-emerged as the defining piece of my thesis - Your Clothing is Still Downloading – a multi dimensional installation which included a live performance by real life and Second Life performers, pre-recorded machinima and video, a live video stream into Second Life, a virtual build of the gallery in Second Life and live projections within the gallery space. The work, which explores identity and desire - was accessible both in the gallery and via a Second Life portal and threw the audiences between both spaces in a perpetual loop. The technical demands of this work on the system often results in a major crash, negating the work in its process.

Each of the main studio works in this research project – Reality Bytes, Byten I –III, Exquisite Corpse, iObject and the Jacksonworks teased out the nature of identity, role play, desire and death through performance, installation, machinima and virtual re-enactment. In the process of performing or displaying these works, the relationship of these new virtual worlds and mixed realities to an art audience was examined and refined. By commencing with the most complex work, Reality Bytes, I was able to test the limits of technology and audience comprehension and engagement and then work backwards to strip down the work to its key elements. The final work in the research project iObject removed the live element completely and explored my digital identity through the negation of self in a virtual world. By completely stripping my self-portrait avatar of all identifiable features and symbols of desire and ego, she was voided, and ultimately challenged the position of identity in this hyper real world. This deconstructed avatar staged a number of sit ins as a three dimensional shadow in the consumer, social and sexual constructions of Second Life – provoking reactions of scorn, threat and complete disregard by observing avatars. Sitting silently in her commodified surroundings, the death of her virtual ego and loss of virtual currency was underscored by the evocative sounds of a Buddhist chant – creating a blur between an act of holiness or menace. In a way, it was the myself as artist role playing myself into a ghost in the machine.

The work annulled the need for the audience's knowledge of its medium (a common problem for SL artists) as the image of a shadow self within a rich virtual environment spoke clearly in its symbols across the void of the real and the virtual. Whilst works like iObject challenged the notion of digital identity, the multi-planed mixed reality performances challenge audiences further via their forced interaction across platforms and into worlds and screens that they may be unfamiliar with. Each time these mixed reality performances were undertaken in this project – the limitations of the system were tested to the extreme. Internet connection, computer graphic capabilities, institutional blocks on Second Life, multiple avatars in the space affecting rezzing and lag (transforming avatars into faceless jerking grey beings) – the act of the performance breaks the technology itself – hence negating not only the self and the avatar self but also the system we are channelling them through.

In your artist practice, concepts like materiality, reality, virtuality and fantasy in contemporary culture are blurred. Moreover, you also create a dialogue between the history of art and new media. I am specifically thinking aboutyour worl Uncomposed (after Titian after Giorgione). Can you tell me more about this work?

- Uncomposed was one of my first works for a long period of time where I moved away from working with a live environment. The work was 'composed' of 3D animation, machinima, and found image mash ups (being the elements of the original master painting).

Made specifically for a group show themed 'Composite', the work deconstructs Giorgione's Sleeping Venus, itself a composite, the landscape and sky being completed by Titian following Giogione's death in 1510. The work was a landmark of its era, reflecting a new shift in modern art with the inclusion of a female nude at its centre. Employing three-dimensional computer graphics and elements of Giorgione's original masterpiece, I replaced his stylised renaissance figure with a fantasised digital body transplanted into an augmented hyper real landscape. In the likeness of her present day artist, the 21st Century Venus will not lie still for her voyeurs, obstinately returning the male gaze from her new digital paradigm, the sleeping Venus awakes. The work also reflects the re-composition of all art works, and all art practices. Obviously, art has never existed in a bubble, as artists we are composites ourselves, of our forbearers, teachers and peers as well as the wealth of information that surrounds us in our everyday lives. In the digital age, of course, this influx of information is a thousand-fold. Where these composites are generally hidden, in Uncomposed they are very obviously exposed in their reassembly.

Your machinima The Fall Girl shows a young girls in bikini falling down a steep cliff over and over again. It seems like cruel punishment taken from the Greek mythology. Can you explain what the video is about?
- It's well-documented that the sexualisation and objectification of women in video games is common place, as is the constant violence against her. Placed as prop, non player, damsel in distress or sub-hero, the female character is rarely a 'player' of any importance. Where female character heroes are in place, they are overtly sexualised, such as the hyper real soft pornography of Lara Croft's female form. The male gaze manifests itself bi-fold in an immersive environment populated by young men invested in hours of play and character's own digital peers.
By removing the game play in between scenes, which when isolated are disturbing in their sharp focus, the viewer becomes critically aware of the hyper- representation of the character and the violence enacted against her. The protagonist is eternally and perpetually punished in an inescapable digital loop, which I first discovered as a never ending glitch in the game. By recreating the flaw and stripping the character to her default 'nudity' The Fall Girl becomes less unfeeling pixelated form and more vulnerable

victim of her portrayed murder, accidental death or futile suicidal escape from her digital fate.

What kind of games and consoles do you like to work with most and why?
- My work on Second Life was obviously predominantly PC based. Whilst I have more recently moved towards the PS3 for entertainment, I am realising its limitations when looking to mod or capture scenes so am currently in the process of transferring all of my gaming practice across to a desktop computer.

When using the PC with Second Life I was particularly interested in the way the physical body related to the on screen action. Initially, moving my virtual body through this digital environment had a strange and unexpected physical effect. Immersing myself in the screen by day, each I night I dreamt in a "Second Life" world – trees, people and buildings streaming past me in a nauseous wave of giddy intoxication. When objects or other avatars made digital contact with me, I noted an odd physical reaction in my own body. I was quick to discover there was a "gut reaction ….a reality in virtual reality" as Lichty said in Hammering the Void. The brain seemed somewhat confused between these two physical planes.

For me, the PS3 does not relay this effect –whether it's because of the proximity of the screen or the physical connection of the hands to the keyboard, the PC tends to give me a more direct access connection to my character and the world she inhabits.

What is your personal relationship with video games? Why are you interested in using video games in your art practice?
- As a child in the 80's I was an avid PC gamer – immersing myself in games such as SimCity and the very adult Leisure Suit Larry in the Land of the Lounge Lizards. Revisiting the game recently I was interested to see the suicide of Larry, which is a theme that permeates in some of my Second Life work, The Fall Girl and my current work in progress Happy Endgame. Death in virtual worlds seems to be a constant provocation. Despite the word game being irrevocably linked with play, fun and light-heartedness, first person

shooters have a dark edge of violence and masochism and our virtual counterparts live on regardless of our own physical deaths.

In my ongoing exploration of digital identity and desire, I began imagining the online virtual world of Second Life and the people who utilise the technology as being in some kind of perpetual movement away from death: a denial as such. In virtual worlds there is no ageing, no rotting of the flesh. Secondarily there exists an eternal life in these new technologies – from forever live Facebook memorials frozen in time, virtual gravesites, dead celebrity avatars and the pun of the Second Life's program name itself. Despite this, every time I log out of a virtual world my avatar dies – a dissolution of pixels disappearing into the black – only to be reborn, unchanged, at the click of a button. These notions inspired my work exquisite corpse dead daddy, shown most recently at James Makin Gallery in Melbourne, which merges rephotographed family snapshots and machinima of a virtual avatar intimately built in my dead father's image. This 21st Century 'exquisite corpse' explores death, memory, loss and the materiality of the body whilst it's flickering images, a digital Dadaism, reflect the processes of the human memory playing out emotions of grief and yearning.

Ironically it was my childhood history with SimCity that propelled my art practice into the game world. I was working with sculptural objects exploring the matrix and the global city and was online researching digital worlds when I stumbled across Sim City and Second Life - nostalgia, curiosity, then critical interest crept in, and my path was redefined! It is a discovery that I find increasingly engaging. As the new cinema and a phenomena of pop culture, games reflect and shape our society and in particular, our young people's desires and interest. I'm looking forward to continuing to work with games and exploring how our own identities merge and fluctuate in virtual worlds...next on the list the new Tomb Raider, a female protagonist, a female writer, and some horrifically realistic death scenes! Stay tuned!

The interview took place in March 2013.

Bruno Martelli and Ruth Gibson: Game Art in England

Based in London, Bruno Martelli and Ruth Gibson work together and often as igloo with international artists, including John McCormick and Adam Nash. Their practice is multifaceted ranging through installation, intervention, virtualisation, film and performance drawing on the multiple layers of reality and unreality. Much of their work is in recreating environments and systems where coding joins hands with choreographies of the body. Their core concept is the intersection between technology and the human spirit, where our ambivalence to technology is explored with originality, humour and intellect. One of their most interesting project is SwanQuake, created in 2007.

SwanQuake combines Tchaikovsky's ballet Swan Lake and the first-person shooter Quake. Is the title meant to be interpreted as part of your "artistic statement", meaning that the boundaries between high-art and popular culture are not as rigid as one might think? That gameplay is the 21st century equivalent of ballet?
BM: It's not really a statement merely a pun - as are many of our titles. We're using a game engine and incorporating dancing avatars. We were originally going to use the Quake Engine at first then Half-life (we we're also going to have a more game like 'Easter eggs' where you could shoot the ballerinas, but we dropped that). But Cynthia Beth Rubin says it better:

"If Games signify popular youth culture, Dance signifies established high Art culture. Putting them together challenges the non-game savvy viewer, and no doubt equally confuses the gamer. But that is the point. Hybrid culture is not just about mixing East and West in a move towards "cultural diversity"'; it is also about mixing strands of culture within the same geographic location. It is about that mix representing generational differences, gender preferences (whether they come from socialization of some other root) and even differences in class and educational background which define expectations of what constitutes leisure time." (Cynthia Beth Rubin)

The boundaries between fine art and popular culture exist, and some forms of art remain elitist and ideas of what 'craft' is are confused, with the skill being in the idea not necessarily in the workmanship. Anyway, we are interested in putting different forms together one's which you wouldn't ordinarily see together or combined. Some people find the need to categorize and notions of art being entertainment can be frowned upon heavily.

"When I first encountered the work of igloo a number of years ago what impressed me most, ironically was not the technology, but the territory that they explored, revealed & developed with that technology. As director of Fieldgate Gallery, I have encountered & am familiar with video art, site-specific installations, & the video game, & have even seen these elements combined together. What I had not seen before was the total eradication of the boundaries between these disciplines, & it is here that igloo's work is genuinely original. The worlds they create are total simulacrums: there is no separation between the invented & the real, the site & the represented, the local & the imagined. It is a territory that is cohesive & singular in language, yet simultaneously is forever folding in on itself. There work engages the particular of the site while undermining its place, the original & point of departure become one in a conceptual unraveling." (Richard Ducker, 2010)

We sometimes show it in an animation context and this crowd is interesting because although we are welcomed with open arms there has been a recent backlash against 3D work because of it's prevalence in the cinema/movies special effects etc, so appreciation of old techniques are trendy again same in film making. In seven years this will probably change again a constant back and forth of what's in and what's out. In some Game Art its people manipulating code, being clever with it and retro, this is also a trend like early interactive media movements. Already interactive design, also 'the conceptual' in modern art maybe starting to appear pretty tired these days.

What were your original goals when you developed SwanQuake? What kind of techniques did you use build it?
BM: We had been working for a number of years on live performance, using media onstage, controllable virtual characters, ASCII cameras and making CD-Roms. We had been experimenting to try and give some sort of control to the audience. We wanted to make some sort of performance that you could give to someone - actually put something it on their hand -or make it so they could have it at home. We thought about video - but its linear and fixed viewpoint, also difficult to deliver on the web. We had been fooling around with mocap - we made a little piece on the web dotdotdot - you can spin the performers around, slow them down, zoom in etc. it breaks the proscenium arch... because its gotta be quick to download, the audio is internet radio and the characters dont have textures and there's no environment. A logical next step was to make a 3d world for the performance that you can navigate. That means a game engine. We conceived SwanQuake as a series, we are working on the other environments now -they are more fantastical. We install Swanquake in galleries because that seems to be the best 'fit' - now we are building the virtual environments into furniture and creating installations- this is to enhance the sense of immersion.

Actually we're using the Unreal Engine - in fact the ancient Unreal Engine 2 Runtime - Unreal 3 wasn't around when we began working, initially we wanted to use the Valve Source which was called the Half-Life 2 engine back then, there was a problem with the code being leaked onto the net - that held up Half-Life back for an age, eventually we had to start building - Unreal hadn't been a choice as the Unreal tournament etc look so horrible. Runtime is great because its small - it comes with absolutely no assets at all. The editor bundled with tournament mean you have to do a big install of game assets, we didn't want any of that. Runtime is a blank slate. Of course the editor is great! Now we're working with Unity and UDK for different pieces...

RG: We used Vicon optical motion capture systems for the avatars in SwanQuake but for other projects we have used many different systems such as Animazoo Gypsy Gyro, Hypervision, Ascension Motion Wireless, Gypsy Exoskeleton and Flock of Birds to name but a few.

You also created an impressive "user manual". However, unlike traditional instructional texts, your intriguing document is a collection of thoughts and ideas about the very notion of Game Art. Was that document "necessary"? I mean, is Game Art such an arcane, esoteric concept that you felt compelled to write a detailed explanation?
BM: Seemed like we could do with something that gave context - galleries get what were doing when we can show them the pieces in another gallery -there's a sort of 'oh yeah I get it...' moment. But if that's not possible we need something else. Also we are often asked to talk about the work and sometimes give workshops, the book is handy for that. Another reason was that most books about videogame art are B/W - we're really visual and wanted to see some colour pix. The User Manual is part of a series - in a way we wanted to get over the bits talking about us and get onto other people. We don't write ourselves so we worked with Scott (the editor) to get a bunch of people to write the essays, we also wanted a variety of opinions. The next book is about the user experience -were are interviewing some artists and commissioning essays.

RG: The manual doesn't tell you how to play the game because there aren't any rules really. The first half is more of a diary about - 'the making of' and there are instructions of how to actually build what we have and contextualise the work a bit. We wanted to de-mystify the complexities to encourage others to have the confidence to try and make work like this themselves. For the second half we invited several writers to offer up essays around the themes. We are just about to start a follow up which will be less about us and more about artists we missed out, ideas of designing experiences.

Are you also gamers? What is your relationship to videogames?
BM: When I was a boy I had a ZX81 and I used to try and write computer games. - that was really hard and the graphics were somewhat limited....later on I used to run a small design house, one of the clients was the Media Museum in Bradford in the UK. They were adding a media section and my company was asked to help curate and do interactive design for the computer games section. Quake II was really new then and I was making a virtual version of the museum as a Quake level for an exhibit about multiplayer gaming. I made the Quake level and tested it from plans without visiting the real place. When I went for a site visit I was amazed that I instinctively knew where to go in the museum - all the spaces were in my body, just from playing the game. I had a light bulb moment and realised that actually 3d environments were actually really great simulations of real places BUT because almost all computer games are based on fantasy spaces we don't realise because we never been in an alien spacecraft or a dungeon to compare the game to the real version. Anyway straight away I thought this would be something to investigate.

RG: We used to paint together - the subject often grew from screen shots taken from games such as Sonic Hedgehog. We embedded silicon chips into the paint for the 'rings'. We started working on a motion capture animation and were talking to Wavefront and SoftImage about ideas we had about making the entirely motion captured work, people, objects, even water - we were in San Francisco and looking at data gloves and VR - which seems to have resurfaced these days with the advent of stereoscopic and 3d. We worked on a project 'end-if' initially in VRML, hilarious which never really got made - but it was the beginnings of works like dotdotdot (an interactive internet radio widget with 6 motion captured characters you can manipulate and choose different genres of music to listen to in the process.) I have ended up working closely with motion capture ever since as performer, coach, supervisor and researcher.

Do contemporary art critics understand Game Art at all? What was the reaction of the art world to complex artworks like SwanQuake?

RG: We're not really that interested. Unless it's someone like English art critic Brain Sewell who can certainly liven up a journey on the tube, even though you may not always agree with him he's definitely worth it. We're into people who make stuff really and what they have to say.

We were pretty apprehensive when EDGE & the The Guardian Games blog said they were coming to review the opening show of SwanQuake: House. We thought the journalists would just not get it. We were pleasantly surprised to read the reviews, in fact we were very happy with them, they got a real sense of the work.

When we started using game engines to make work one of our first projects was exhibited on a large scale at ISEA/Zero1 in San Jose and Bill Viola was the key note at the conference that year. Many colleagues were in the front few rows of the audience and immediately turned round to us when Viola starting speaking about his new Night Journey (his game environment). I think then it dawned on us that hey, people will accept this artform soon enough if Bill does it. He made video art ok so maybe he'll do the same for this genre or at least art using game tools?

Have you been inspired by other Game Artists?

RG: Not really or should I say not yet, maybe Damiano Colacito because his work is exquisite and hes been making real versions of virtual objects for a long time...also sculptor Oswan Gong who uses a weird photorealistic texture mapping technique, and Richard Wentworth for his playfulness, Doshin the Giant on the GameCube and the Space Channel 5, the Dreamcast game.

BM: So far I prefer games to game art, almost nothing compares the thrill of Half-Life intro sequence, but you have to mention the n+n Corsino and Dear Esther by Dan Pinchbeck. As for 'regular' artists say Xavier Veilhan! Right now our Australian colleagues Adan Nash and John McCormick (SquareTangle) are doing some amazing things with domes - when we first started working with them on SwanQuake it was inspiring to see the projects they had previously made.

In the "Tales of the Forest" exhibition that took place at the Virserum Art Hall in Sweden (9/5 -5/12 2010), you are showing a piece called Summerbranch. How would you describe it?
-Summerbranch is a 3d environment which evokes an English forest and has camouflaged characters hidden in it. We made it and a series if other works including video and lenticular prints, during a residency in the New Forest in the UK. Usually it's a large video projection, with a wooden interface modelled from a virtual tree stump, with wooden trackball and buttons. We've always been obsessed with computer games trees, these ones we had to grow from virtual seeds. We talked to the company who made the software about real models of their trees - it had never occurred to them to try!...Like in all our work, the audio is important, surround sound of forest foley made by one of collaborators Adam Nash. We were very interested in movement / stillness and camouflage techniques when we made the piece - its been shown many times now, some people find it relaxing but others find it quite unnerving, it looks to me old fashioned (we made it in 2005) but somehow it keeps its own aesthetic. What I like to see sometimes is the essential falseness of virtual worlds, I love to see how round surfaces are represented by flat polygonal objects, the other thing is, how in nature, green plants in the sun have the same brightness as peak green RGB values.

The interview took place in May 2010.

www.ingramcontent.com/pod-product-compliance
Lightning Source LLC
Chambersburg PA
CBHW020444220526
45464CB00002B/843